DEVELOPING
TEACHER
LEADERS

DEVELOPING TEACHER LEADERS

HOW TEACHER LEADERSHIP ENHANCES SCHOOL SUCCESS

FRANK CROWTHER
STEPHEN S. KAAGAN
MARGARET FERGUSON
LEONNE HANN

FOREWORD BY
ANDY HARGREAVES

CORWIN PRESS, INC.
A Sage Publications Company
Thousand Oaks, California

For information:

Corwin Press, Inc.
A Sage Publications Company
2455 Teller Road
Thousand Oaks, California 91320
E-mail: order@corwinpress.com

Sage Publications Ltd.
6 Bonhill Street
London EC2A 4PU
United Kingdom

Sage Publications India Pvt. Ltd.
M-32 Market
Greater Kailash I
New Delhi 110 048 India

Printed in the United States of America

Library of Congress Cataloging-in-Publication Data

Developing teacher leaders: How teacher leadership enhances school success / by Frank Crowther . . . [et al.].
    p. cm.
Includes bibliographical references and index.
  ISBN 0-7619-4561-X — ISBN 0-7619-4562-8 (pbk.)
  1. Teacher effectiveness. 2. Educational leadership. I. Crowther, Frank, 1942-
  LB1025.3 .D487 2002
  371.1'06—dc21

                           2002000148

This book is printed on acid-free paper.

03   04   05   06   07   7   6   5   4   3

Acquisitions Editor: Rachel Livsey
Editorial Assistant: Phyllis Cappello
Production Editor: Olivia Weber
Typesetter: Rebecca Evans
Indexer: Pamela Van Huss
Cover Designer: Michael Dubowe
Production Artist: Janet Foulger

Contents

Foreword

Educational leadership is at a crossroads. Effective leadership in schools and of schools has always been crucial for effective teaching and learning in classrooms. But in the early years of a new century, leadership matters more than ever. The demands on leadership are increasing: External accountability calls for endless interactions with an expanding range of parents and other partners, and internal responsibility means that leaders need to know more and do more about students' learning and with the ever-changing knowledge base on which learning is built. At the same time, in a world of constant pressure for school achievement, endless shifts and reversals in policy demands—and repeated breakthroughs in brain-based learning, literacy strategies, and other learning developments—leaders must be able to build capacity in themselves and others to respond swiftly, knowledgeably, and responsibly, to the constant currents of uncertainty and change.

For many leaders, the demands of leadership have become just too demanding. Principals who are ageing baby boomers frequently choose to retire early because of stress, burnout, or disillusionment with the impact on their lives and their work of years of mandated reform (Day & Bakioglu, 1996). Middle-level school leaders, such as secondary school department heads, are faring no better. Their stress levels are often the highest in teaching, because delegated pressures to implement external reforms have rarely been balanced by any sense of power, time, or discretion to implement effectively or to innovate by themselves (Dinham & Scott, 1997; Troman & Woods, 2000). Women leaders can be especially vulnerable, as impossible requirements or unpalatable demands stretch their ethics of caring to the limit—leading them to feel guilty about letting their colleagues down and emotionally alone in their efforts to avoid doing so (Beatty, 2000; Blackmore, 1996).

The result is that, in the midst of a massive demographic exodus in school leadership, new candidates for leadership who care about leading, want to lead, and feel able to lead in current circumstances are as rare as mosquitoes in the snow. Educational leadership is becoming a vacant lot, always up for rent.

Teaching, too, is in crisis, staring tragedy in the face. The demographic exodus is no smaller for teachers than it is for leaders. And after a decade of relentless reform in a climate of shaming and blaming teachers for perpetuating poor standards, the attractiveness of teaching as a profession has faded fast among potential new recruits. Teaching has to compete much harder against other professions for high-caliber candidates than it did in the days of the baby boomers—when able women were led to feel that only nursing and secretarial work were viable options. Teaching may not yet have reverted to being an occupation for "unmarriageable women and unsaleable men," as Waller (1932, p. 379) described it, but many American inner cities now run their school systems with high numbers of uncertified teachers. And the teacher-recruitment crisis in England has led some schools to move to a 4-day week. In the Canadian province of Ontario, hard-nosed and hard-headed reform strategies have led, in a single year, to a decrease in applications to teacher education programs in faculties of education by 20 to 25 percent and to a drop in grade level of accepted applicants.

Teaching today is highly complex work, requiring the highest standards of professional practice to perform it well (Hargreaves & Goodson, 1996). As Frank Crowther, Steve Kaagan, Margaret Ferguson, and Leonne Hann note in this excellent book, it is the core profession, the key agent of change in today's knowledge society. Teachers are the midwives of that knowledge society. Without them, without their competence, our future will be malformed and stillborn. In the United States, George W. Bush's educational slogan has been to leave no child behind. What is clear today, in general, and in this book, in particular, is that leaving no child behind means leaving no teacher leader behind, either.

Amid all the despair and danger that I have outlined, however, there remain great hope and reasons for optimism about a future of learning that is tied in its vision to an empowering, imaginative, and inclusive vision for teaching and for leading as well. The educational-standards movement shows signs of overreaching itself as people start to complain about teacher shortages in schools and the loss of creativity and inspiration in classrooms (Hargreaves, Earl, Moore, & Manning, 2001). There is growing international support for the resumption of more humane middle-years philosophies in the early years of secondary school that put priority on community and engagement, alongside curriculum content and academic achievement. And governments almost everywhere are beginning to speak more positively about teachers and teaching—bestowing honor and respect where blame and contempt have prevailed in the recent past.

There is a massive renewal of interest in educational leadership, too, with American foundations investing vast resources in leadership training initiatives, and a National College for School Leadership being created in England to organize and orchestrate the whole span of educational leadership for an entire nation. There is much to be excited and optimistic about in the future of teaching and leading.

Developing Teacher Leaders is grounded in this fundamental sense of optimism but not naively so. It brings the divided worlds of teaching and leading together in a conceptually sophisticated and strategically powerful way. The worst move we can make at this crossroads that defines the future of teaching and leading is to delineate endless standards and competences for future teachers, to devise and deliver countless courses and certificates in leadership training for school principals, and to create more and more contrived career pathways between the two. All this would do is perpetuate the overregulation of teaching and leading as well as maintain an historically unproductive division between them.

Instead, Crowther, Kaagan, Ferguson, and Hann show the intimate connection that exists between teaching and leading, realistically as well as rhetorically. In doing so, they demonstrate not only what can be created but also what already exists. When leadership is conceived as principalship, then really effective principals can bring about successful innovation, turn underperforming schools around, and even sustain change over 3 to 5 years. But typically, when top-level leaders move on, the focus shifts, the ownership of change leaves with the departing leaders, and their successors then reverse the trend, neglecting what has been achieved or even undoing it as they try, like an unwanted stepfather or stepmother, to put their own stamp on the family they have inherited (Hargreaves & Fink, 2000). Currently, few things succeed less than leadership succession, and that, as Crowther, Kaagan, Ferguson, and Hann make clear, is because the potential for lasting leadership has been subverted by locking up leadership in the roles and behaviors of a few individuals.

In this outstanding book, however, the authors demonstrate the power in practice of a more distributed or distributive concept of leadership (Handy, 1994; Spillane, Halverson, & Diamond, 2001) that includes and engages teachers and others, as well as those in more strictly administrative roles. They demonstrate, through real examples and vignettes from across the world, how such distributed leadership works in practice as teachers are allowed and encouraged to take charge of profound learning initiatives in their own schools and beyond.

The authors' concept of parallel leadership is especially important in its articulation of the connection between teacher leadership and principal leadership through mutual respect, shared sense of purpose, and encouragement of individual variations and differences. Nor are the visions of learning embedded in this parallel leadership confined to narrow definitions of measurable achievement; they encompass deep cognitive learning as well as the social, moral, aesthetic, and spiritual aspects of learning and development. Crowther, Kaagan, Ferguson, and Hann call for leadership that builds powerful, caring, and inclusive communities that make students into dynamic learning machines. As expressed in the Preface, they want teachers and leaders for schools that are more than bundles of standards and competencies—for schools that are "dynamic sources of inspiration," for schools that are "intellectually vibrant, morally disciplined, and aesthetically stimulating" (p. xiv).

Developing Teacher Leaders provides an intellectually stimulating and practically realizable vision of leadership in schools that is inclusive and inspiring, stretching far beyond the command and control models of change that have dominated educational reforms for more than a decade. If educational improvement is to last, it must depend on more than a few leaders whose departure leads to the improvements' demise. It must be built not on the capacities of individual *leaders* but rather on powerful communities of teacher *leadership* that continue to make and sustain change with, and alongside, administrators—and even after those administrators abandon them. In theory, and in a set of provocative, practical exercises for teachers and their colleagues, this is the vision that *Developing Teacher Leaders* articulates so successfully.

The authors are not just armchair theorists. Their lifework has demonstrated a dedication to working energetically, collaboratively, and successfully with educational practitioners of all kinds. There is no idea in this book that has not been seen and witnessed, tried and tested in the work they have done.

In the quest to improve schools, narrow the learning gap between privileged and marginalized groups, and restore reward and respect to the teaching profession, few things matter more at the moment than a renewal of leadership. *Developing Teacher Leaders* takes this vital agenda for leadership renewal in an imaginative direction that will challenge all who read it to think about their own and others' leadership, and about the future of school leadership, very differently.

— Andy Hargreaves
Professor in the Department of Theory and Policy Studies in Education,
Ontario Institute for Studies in Education, University of Toronto

Preface

Knowledge workers will give the emerging knowledge society its character, its leadership, its social profile. They may not be the ruling class of the knowledge society, but they are already its leading class. And in their characteristics, social position, values, and expectations, they differ fundamentally from any group in history that has ever occupied the leading position.

— Peter Drucker (1994, p. 64)

Why This Book and Why Now?

The challenge Drucker poses for knowledge-based professions is daunting. One can only surmise that professions, as we currently know them, will look very different in 20 years and that the underlying principles of our own profession, teaching, will be called into question at least as much as those of other professions. Our view in writing this book is that the teaching profession is potentially well placed to become what Drucker calls a "leading class" of the emerging postindustrial world. We make this assertion with confidence because inherent to teaching is the kind of leadership that society will require in the years ahead.

Not long ago, we leaned toward the prevailing perspective that the teaching profession was in decline. Confronted with evidence of the lessening interest in teaching as a career and with incessant media reporting on education as a problem—school violence, unsatisfactory student achievement, inadequate educational funding, loss of confidence in public education generally—we had to struggle, as have so many educators, to maintain optimism and confidence that teaching had the positive future that we believed it did. Our optimism was strengthened by the research for this book and by the dialogue with educators across the globe that has been part of it.

We worked for 5 years with an array of the extraordinary individuals who bring life to our schools. As researchers, we engaged teachers and school principals in contexts as diverse as a Midwestern American city and an outback Australian bush town. As scholars, we searched for meaning through presentations at international conferences and in the staff rooms of elementary and secondary schools. As our journey progressed, we became increasingly optimistic that the coming decades will be shaped, more than anything else, by qualities that are currently obscured in the work of the teaching profession—but are, nonetheless, present and waiting to be uncovered and used.

This book is for people who believe it is critically important to enrich the leadership of our schools. People who suspect that the models of school leadership that dominate worldwide are weary, worn, and inadequate. People who believe that the teaching profession's growth for the past several decades has been severely stunted and is overdue, not just for revitalization but also for renaissance. People who believe that the teaching profession must, in fact, be the centerpiece of the emerging knowledge society, creating schools that are dynamic sources of inspiration in a world that, for many, is confusing and alienating.

In the context of current school reform efforts, this book is also for beginning and seasoned teachers, novice and experienced administrators, and dedicated community and business leaders; in other words, for those who want schools to be centers of learning—intellectually vibrant, morally disciplined, and aesthetically stimulating—and who know that teachers are, ultimately, the primary moving force toward effecting these ends. We write, too, for educators and citizen leaders who believe that the development of people's human capabilities will, in the long run, produce greater achievement gains than accountability strategies, including large-scale, externally driven testing programs and privatization initiatives.

The Teachers as Leaders Framework (Table 1.1, page 4) represents the essential source of our optimism and confidence. We have seen it exemplified in a wide range of contexts and have witnessed its capacity to enhance not just school outcomes but also the quality of life in school communities. Yet, we are realists. The past 40 years have not been kind to the teaching profession. The mindset that schools have little effect on children's life chances, a widely accepted interpretation of the Coleman report (Coleman, 1966), promoted policies that we believe minimized the work of teachers worldwide.

This mindset will not disappear overnight, as a series of recent, nationally commissioned reports have made clear. In the United States, during the past 2 decades, these included the reports by the Holmes Group (1986), the Carnegie Forum on Education and the Economy (1986), and the Education Commission of the States (1983). The "I'm just a teacher" syndrome that has come internationally to dominate many teachers' self-concept will also not disappear in the short term. Nor will the diminished image and esteem of the teaching profession.

The Teacher as Leaders Framework captures a view of the teaching profession that stands in stark contrast to the view that has come to dominate so much professional and lay thinking during this time. It makes clear that many teachers who currently work in our schools have leadership qualities that have not previously been recognized and that, if actualized, could transform not only schools but also communities. And it points to a new concept—one that we call *parallel leadership*. This represents a major rethinking of teacher-principal relationships for successful schooling and, in so doing, shows the way for schools to become the centerpiece of the emerging knowledge society.

A Different Approach to Teacher Leadership

This book is different because it proposes that educational leadership for the emerging postindustrial world must embrace the leadership capabilities of teachers. When we use the term *teacher leadership,* we refer not solely to professionalism, enthusiasm, passion, and commitment. To be sure, schools need all these from their classroom teachers. But what we are talking about is a form of leadership suited to the imperative that schools transform themselves and, in so doing, demonstrate for communities how that transformation can be managed positively and effectively. Ultimately, teacher leadership, as we intend it, is about action that transforms teaching and learning in a school, that ties school and community together on behalf of learning, and that advances social sustainability and quality of life for a community. All these elements are part of the portfolio of teacher leaders. Thus this book is different, not just because we assert the need for new forms of leadership in our schools, but also because we define teacher leadership in detail.

As authors, we take a radically different view from that articulated by many authors who have published works on leadership in recent decades. Such books reflect on past or present leadership practices, or purport to show the way to the future, or articulate important techniques for aspiring leaders. An increasing number draw their wisdom from the lives of historic figures, such as Moses, Jesus, Abraham Lincoln, Queen Elizabeth I, Mahatma Gandhi, and Sir Winston Churchill. The focus of most of the works is on business leadership, to a lesser extent on public affairs leadership, and to a much lesser extent still, on educational and school leadership.

The impetus for this widespread interest in leadership stems from a number of factors. A major one appears to be an increasingly widespread belief that we do not have enough leadership, or we have the wrong kind, or a combination of the two. In the case of educational leadership, it is probably fair to say that both dearth and misdirection are in play.

Few of the many leadership books acknowledge that the main aim of education is learning. Even fewer recognize that teachers are the main human instruments of this learning. Beare's (2001) assertion that "Who the teacher of the future will be and how she will operate is certain to be influenced by the emerging work-style of knowledge workers" (p. 181) and Drucker's (1994) futuristic analysis that "education will become the center of the knowledge society and the school its key institution" (p. 66) are obscured in most of the treatises on leadership we have reviewed. The notion that teachers can be, should be, and frequently are leaders, in every sense of the word—as they pass along knowledge to the next generation—is not, unfortunately, a significant feature of educational leadership as construed in the literature.

Stated differently, the 21st century will not be the same as the 20th. Even our basic concepts of democracy are evolving and changing. Esteemed American educator John Goodlad (as cited in Goldberg, 2000) stated recently that "the workplace will not survive unless we educate people for democracy . . . and there needs to be a profound rethinking of what 21st century democracy requires of the schools" (p. 84). He pointed to the unequivocal importance of leadership roles for schools that have not yet been recognized. Our book represents a partial response to Goodlad's challenge.

We seek a dramatic reformulation of the way people think about educational leadership. We argue not only for new leadership fabric, but also for new ways of sewing the pieces together and, ultimately, for a completely new look and feel to the educational leadership quilt. In contending that education is about student learning—about intellectual, moral, emotional, and spiritual growth and development and, by association, about the teaching that supports that learning—this book places in the background the array of political, organizational, and societal issues that frequently eclipse our attention as professionals. We regard compelling policy concerns—such as privatization of schools, large-scale assessment efforts, alternative financing strategies, and collective bargaining and governance structures—as subsidiary to leadership that has the capacity to directly affect students, their well-being as well as their achievement.

Moreover, teacher leadership appears to be inseparable from successful school reform as it is currently envisioned. This book offers strong evidence that school-based interventions, involving teacher leadership and parallel leadership, can produce enhanced educational outcomes. This evidence comes from our 5 years of sustained inquiry into the subject as well as from research by others in Australia (Crowther, Hann, & McMaster, 2001) and the United States (King & Newmann, 2000; Muncey & McQuillan, 1996; Newmann & Wehlage, 1995). In proposing a definitive concept of teacher leadership, in projecting a central role for the teaching profession in the knowledge society of the future, and in linking teacher leadership to deliberate and sustained school reform, this book is distinctive.

The Teachers as Leaders Research Project, 1996 to 2000

The frameworks for teacher leadership and parallel leadership that are the foundation of this book stem from research conducted in three phases over 5 years, with support from three research funding agencies. The first two phases were completed in Queensland, Australia, and the third was undertaken as part of an Australia-wide project with links to Michigan. Professor Frank Crowther, Director of the Leadership Research Institute at the University of Southern Queensland, was the leader of the overall research project. Margaret Ferguson initiated the phase-one study and participated in the phase-two study. Leonne Hann was the principal field researcher for phases two and three. External validation exercises were undertaken through two procedures:

- Critical analysis of phase-one and phase-two outcomes, through an international on-line conference convened by the Australian Council for Educational Administration in September, 1999

- Face-to-face analysis of phase-three outcomes with a range of educational groups in Michigan. Professor Steve Kaagan of Michigan State University provided advice during phase two and three of the Australian research and coordinated the Michigan validation studies.

The research began in disadvantaged communities. The principal purpose was to illuminate the work of extraordinary teachers whose impact on their schools and communities had won the acclaim of their principals and colleagues. Some had addressed complex issues involving rural isolation. Others had succeeded in situations of serious prejudice and cultural conflict in Aboriginal communities, while still others had confronted the results of high-level unemployment in communities that suffered its ill effects for generations. From those early explorations, we were able to identify what we regard as the essentials of teacher leadership.

A second focus involved the exploration of our emerging Teacher Leadership Framework in schools where documented evidence existed of significantly enhanced student achievement. From this aspect of the research, we formulated the notion of parallel leadership and developed a model of the way that parallel leadership affects school capacity building.

A third emphasis involved insights into the role of principals in creating and sustaining parallel leadership and in nurturing teacher leadership as a basis for school revitalization.

Organization of the Book

Developing Teacher Leaders is both conceptual and developmental. In synthesizing our inquiry in two countries, it describes teacher leadership, parallel leadership, and ways that these ideas engender improved outcomes, including student achievement, teacher esteem and morale, and community confidence and appreciation. In providing a range of relevant professional learning exercises, it also offers readers a platform for engaging the concepts of teacher leadership and parallel leadership in their own schools.

In Chapter 1, we explain the concept of teacher leadership that emerged from our research. Central to this chapter are a definition of teacher leadership and a framework that outlines the main elements of teacher leadership. These derive from case research done during the three phases of the Teachers as Leaders Project and numerous discussions with teachers and others from around the world over several years.

Chapter 2 presents five premises derived from our research that we believe provide new direction for the teaching profession in the emerging knowledge society. A simple but profound conclusion emerges from the first of these premises: All the essential elements of significant leadership theories are present in the work of some, if not all, classroom teachers. As remarkable as this assertion may be, these elements do not represent the sum total of teacher leadership, nor do existing theories capture the full power of teacher leadership. Rather, teacher leadership has an extra dimension that distinguishes it from other leadership forms, namely, a focus on schoolwide excellence in teaching, learning, and assessment, a concept that is fundamental to successful school reform.

Chapter 3 introduces a new idea, parallel leadership. Parallel leadership is necessary if school vision and classroom practices are to be aligned, and if school revitalization is to be sustained over time. Parallel leadership, as we define it, encourages a relatedness between teacher leaders and principal leaders that enables the knowledge-generating capacity of schools to be activated and sustained. Our Diagram Linking Parallel Leadership and Successful School Reform (Figure 3.1), drawn from our research and inseparable from parallel leadership, is in Chapter 3.

Chapter 4 outlines the role of the school principal in nurturing teacher leadership. We discuss seven challenges that derive from an analysis of the roles of the principals in our case studies of successful parallel leadership.

Ideas Into Action Through Development Exercises

Developing Teacher Leaders also provides a basis for the professional learning of educators seeking to enrich the leadership of their schools. Complementing the concepts in Chapters 1 to 4 is a kind of development manual which constitutes Chapters 5 and 6. The ideas presented in these final chapters, contain the substance of seminar programs that readers can use to their advantage to become teacher leaders. They give readers many of the benefits that participants in highly successful leadership seminars run by one of the authors receive. The ideas were refined through interactions with two groups. The first comprised educators who had been identified as teacher leaders. The second comprised principals and other administrators who desired to nurture teacher leadership in their schools.

The 14 exercises, introduced in Chapter 5 and presented in Chapter 6, have three common qualities. First, they are experiential—they involve doing, not just reading about, listening to, and critiquing ideas. Second, they involve participants' analyses of their own thought processes and emotions as part of the experience of professional learning. Third, they relate directly to the core concepts of the book, namely, teacher leadership and parallel leadership.

The exercises are designed to be used primarily by teachers and principals in schools aspiring to build their leadership capacity. There are explicit and detailed directions for each one. The exercises can be completed without external facilitation, although with qualified outside help, the impact will likely be greater in some schools. Having completed the exercises, preferably as part of a collaborative, schoolwide process, participants should be well equipped to undertake further development work on their own.

Appendix A contains a description of the research methodology that has underpinned our 5 years of developmental work. The three stages of the research are outlined, along with sample research data that indicate our confidence in a relationship between the leadership concepts and processes featured in this book and the enhancement of educational outcomes. A list of the Australian case study schools is also included.

Appendix B recounts discussions held in Michigan with teacher leaders and other educators concerning the main ideas in the book.

Acknowledgments

This book is the result of a substantial collaborative effort among researchers and practicing educators across two continents and 5 years. We owe colleague Peter Olsen, who coordinated the initial stages of our research, a particular debt of gratitude, along with the two Queensland, Australia, school principals, Peter Baker and Neil Mahoney, who, in early 1995, observed a number of extraordinary developments in their seriously disadvantaged school communities that resulted from initiatives by classroom teachers. They approached the Leadership Research Institute at the University of Southern Queensland for assistance in exploring and documenting those developments. Because of their professional curiosity and commitment, the *Teachers as Leaders* project was born.

The editorial critique and advice offered by Dorothy Bramston, Dorothy Andrews, Marilyn Katzenmeyer, Gayle Moller, John McMaster,

Mark Dawson, Marian Lewis, Charles Webber, and Rod Linhart was immensely valuable. Educators at various locations in Queensland, in Michigan, USA, and in Alberta, Canada, reviewed our proposals and responded to them with valuable insights. Special mention is made of the contribution by staff members of Goondiwindi High School, Queensland, whose schoolwide reform efforts gave credence to the key concepts in this book.

Finally, the 5 years of research on which this book is based were made possible with funding support from the Australian Research Council, the Queensland Department of Education, and the Australian Commonwealth Department of Education, Training and Youth Affairs.

Concluding Comment

Basic to our thinking is that the world is not standing still, nor will the future resemble the present, let alone the past. The Teachers as Leaders Framework that is central to this book, and the related notion of parallel leadership, will undoubtedly evolve into new forms and acquire new meanings. Also basic to our thinking is the validity of Drucker's assertion, which introduces this preface: In the emerging postindustrial world, leadership will be assumed by knowledge workers. We assert that teachers are ideally placed to become the central knowledge-generating profession. The concepts and the developmental activities that make up *Developing Teacher Leaders* reflect not only our optimism but also our view that for members of the teaching profession, the journey into the postindustrial world will be compelling.

— Frank Crowther and Steve Kaagan

About the Authors

Frank Crowther is an internationally respected scholar and researcher in educational management and leadership. He is Professor and Director of the Leadership Research Institute at the University of Southern Queensland, Australia. In 1997, he was awarded the Gold Medal of the Australian Council for Educational Administration in recognition of his services to educational leadership.

Stephen S. Kaagan is Professor of Education at Michigan State University. His teaching interests are leadership, organizational analysis, and administrative practice. He has been honored with several awards, including membership in the Royal Society for the Encouragement of Arts, Manufactures and Commerce, London; and honorary doctorates from Williams College in Massachusetts and Green Mountain College in Vermont. He most recently authored *Leadership Games: Experiential Learning for Organizational Development* (1999, Sage).

Margaret Ferguson is District Manager of Education Services at Education Queensland. Her work focuses on capacity building, curriculum leadership, and pedagogical enhancement in schools. She has worked extensively in teacher leader development.

Leonne Hann is Senior Research Associate in the Leadership Research Institute at the University of Southern Queensland. She has participated in national research projects in school innovation. Her recently completed postgraduate study deals with teacher leadership and successful school reform.

PART 1

Defining Ideas

Teachers as Leaders
Emergence of a New Paradigm

Within every school there is a sleeping giant of teacher leader-ship, which can be a strong catalyst for making change. By using the energy of teacher leaders as agents of school change, the reform of public education will stand a better chance of building momentum.

— Marilyn Katzenmeyer and Gayle Moller (1996, p. 2)

Needed: A New Paradigm of the Teaching Profession

Even a cursory reading of the educational literature leads to the conclusion that the way the teaching profession is currently viewed is ill founded and out-of-date—in a word, wrong. Although the challenges confronting schools worldwide are greater than ever before, and many teachers possess capabilities, talents, and formal credentials more sophisticated than ever before, the responsibility and authority accorded teachers has not grown or changed significantly in decades.

Thus a new paradigm of the teaching profession is needed, one that recognizes both the capacity of the profession to provide desperately needed school revitalization and the striking potential of teachers to provide new forms of leadership in schools and communities. The Teachers as Leaders Framework (Table 1.1) that represents the core of this chapter—and, indeed, of this book—substantiates the assertion that teacher leadership is an idea whose time has come. This assertion was advanced by Katzenmeyer and Moller (1996) in the first edition of

Table 1.1 The Teachers as Leaders Framework

Teacher Leaders

Convey convictions about a better world by
- articulating a positive future for students
- showing a genuine interest in students' lives
- contributing to an image of teachers as professionals who make a difference
- gaining respect and trust in the broader community
- demonstrating tolerance and reasonableness in difficult situations

Strive for authenticity in their teaching, learning, and assessment practices by
- creating learning experiences related to students' needs
- connecting teaching, learning, and assessment to students' futures
- seeking deep understanding of tacit teaching and learning processes
- valuing teaching as a key profession in shaping meaning systems

Facilitate communities of learning through organization-wide processes by
- encouraging a shared, schoolwide approach to pedagogy (teaching, learning, and assessment)
- approaching professional learning as consciousness raising about complex issues
- facilitating understanding across diverse groups while also respecting individual differences
- synthesizing new ideas out of colleagues' dialogues and activities

Confront barriers in the school's culture and structures by
- testing the boundaries rather than accepting the status quo
- engaging administrators as potential sources of assistance and advocacy
- accessing political processes in and out of the school
- standing up for children, especially marginalized or disadvantaged individuals or groups

Table 1.1 Continued

Teacher Leaders

Translate ideas into sustainable systems of action by

- organizing complex tasks effectively
- maintaining focus on issues of importance
- nurturing networks of support
- managing issues of time and pressure through priority setting

Nurture a culture of success by

- acting on opportunities for others to gain success and recognition
- adopting a no-blame attitude when things go wrong
- creating a sense of community identity and pride

their landmark publication, *Awakening the Sleeping Giant: Leadership Development for Teachers.* They claimed that the teachers have the potential to exercise new and dynamic leadership in schools, thereby enhancing the possibility of social reform. They introduced the metaphor of a sleeping giant to illustrate not just the current dormant status of teacher leadership but also the power it might exert if aroused.

In the 5 years since publication of *Awakening the Sleeping Giant,* teacher leadership has drawn considerable attention worldwide and has acquired a degree of legitimacy in the educational literature if not in educational practice. But what does *teacher leadership* mean? Sherrill (1999) has pointed to the ambiguity surrounding the term in the literature, asserting that "teacher leaders are referred to as clinical faculty, clinical educators, teachers-in-residence, master teachers, lead teachers, and clinical supervisors" (p. 57). In our view, teachers' proficiency in areas of specialized competence, such as those identified by Sherrill, may point to the growing maturity of the profession, but it does not directly provide direction for teachers aspiring to lead school reform. New, dynamic, defensible conceptions of teacher leadership are required as a matter of immense professional urgency. The search for this new paradigm informs this chapter.

Chapter 1 is an optimistic and confident assessment of the teaching profession. It is grounded in highly successful, real-life school practices. It presents a view of educational leadership that is idealistic, realistic, and suited to the complex needs of school communities in a rapidly changing world.

Two Snapshots

To begin, we profile two schools where teacher leaders have exercised distinctive forms of leadership to shape meaning for their students and communities.

Snapshot One: Greenhills State High School

Greenhills has 500 students and is situated in a small, economically depressed rural town. Because it is attractive in many ways, the casual visitor to Greenhills could be forgiven for not discerning that the surrounding community has endured a long-term slump in its primary industrial base, that it has one of the highest levels of economic disadvantage in the nation, and that as many as three generations of some families have experienced persistent unemployment.

According to a veteran teacher at the school, students used to "come to school with their shoulders drooped." It was in this context of limited opportunity and low levels of motivation that teacher leaders undertook to provide the material out of which success stories are made.

Where it all began is still not entirely clear. Perhaps it was the Student Aspirations Program, through which a small group of teachers built a system for student mentoring and peer support. This involved identifying students' interests or talents as a starting point for building self-esteem and proficiency and, ultimately, for broadening their horizons for future endeavors. Over the years, the Student Aspirations Program became part of the fabric of the school, changing regularly as new teachers, with new interests and capacities, joined the community. Conceivably, it was only when the school motto—*success breeds success*—began to infiltrate the thinking of the whole school community that students' expectations and self-belief started to change.

A second possibility is that credit for initiating the turnaround should be assigned to the current principal. Among his considerable talents is his ability to convince students that personal demeanor—dress, speech, manners—is very important to their achieving enhanced levels of academic and post-school success. He also insisted that every achievement, no matter how small, or in what field, was worthy of celebration. Thus he had no difficulty convincing Nancy and Lisa, two young teachers, of the impact of their public speaking initiatives and organized-sports competitions on student motivation, self-expectation, and school pride. Nor did he have difficulty accommodating the school resources committee's recommendation that finances be made available to facilitate access to on-line career information for students and the community to improve career opportunities for all.

The positive effects of synergistic leadership at Greenhills State High are numerous. First, the school has achieved marked recognition for its academic, cultural, and sporting successes, having been honored in a statewide showcasing competition. Second, it has undertaken significant educational innovations in which teachers have challenged themselves to improve their teaching practices. Third, community surveys indicated that it has become regarded as the center of local community life to an extent seldom achieved by a high school.

The teacher leaders we observed at Greenhills were able to articulate clearly their goals and strategies. They spoke convincingly of the "we can do anything" mindset of the student body, the inseparability of school and community, the sense of reward that goes with overcoming immense odds, and the teamwork of the teachers, matched by the facilitative support of the principal. They regarded their school as unique, and they treasured that uniqueness, despite, or maybe because of, the human disadvantage, and even despair, out of which it had emerged.

The question we asked ourselves as we left Greenhills was, "Could this dynamic leadership come from elsewhere in the community or does it point to something distinctive about the teaching profession?" Certainly, our analysis of the leadership processes in place at Greenhills, supported by the views of teachers and school administrators, is that the magic of Greenhills resides substantially in the power of teachers—through their pedagogical and community-building practices—to transform their schools and enrich their communities.

Snapshot Two: Sunbeach Elementary and Middle School

Sunbeach has 300 students and is located in a small town that nestles in tropical bushland. The questions asked and answered there were, "Can a classroom teacher single handedly inspire and coordinate a literacy program that enhances student achievement across an entire school? If so, what sort of leadership does it take?" The lessons learned from this remarkable story say a great deal about teacher leadership and its potential to contribute to the revitalization of schools:

Loretta returned from the professional development day buoyed by new ideas and possibilities. What she had observed was an integrated approach to literacy that built on basic skills and seemed ideally suited to the needs of students in her remote rural school, with its large number of transient students. As a learning support teacher, however, she had no formal authority on which to build and sustain a schoolwide innovation. But Loretta's boundless enthusiasm for literacy innovation was matched by her determination. She had energy, passion, and optimism. And she was a thoughtful educator, well respected by her colleagues. She immediately shared her ideas and enthusiasm with the principal, Paul, who encouraged her to test them out with the school staff. The school's curriculum team was more questioning, drawing attention to likely incompatibilities with teaching styles, the extreme difficulty of creating a schoolwide approach to literacy, limited resources, the absence of a training program, and the largely untried nature of the innovation itself.

A colleague, Claire, told Loretta about an advertised funding opportunity and coordinated, under difficult circumstances, the preparation of a successful grant application on her behalf. In a matter of weeks, Loretta had an implementation plan drafted, a training strategy designed, a community communications process in operation, and a school management team in place.

The communications process was particularly innovative, enabling parents to gain access on-line to weekly reports on their children's progress and to reciprocate with information they regarded as relevant. For many parents, particularly those of non-English-speaking students, this aspect of the program provided practical interaction with the school that was unprecedented. Six months later, authoritative testing, conducted with the assistance of a nearby university, provided clear evidence that students' literacy levels had improved. The teachers and principal decided to expand the initiative.

The exceptional success of the Sunbeach literacy program (see Appendix A for details), sustained over time and across grade levels, can be linked to a number of factors. Among them were Loretta's indisputable personal dynamism and drive to address a glaring student need in the school; a professional learning experience that made its mark; the political advocacy of her colleague, Claire; the strong facilitative support of the principal, Paul; a school staff open to suggestions; the availability of funds; external advice and encouragement at critical junctures from a neighboring university; a high degree of task orientation and organizational capacity on the part of a teacher leader and her colleagues; and a district director noted for his entrepreneurial stance.

The pervasive view of the school staff was that, without Loretta's inspiration, conviction, and organizational skill—and without Claire's support in confronting barriers—they would not have achieved anything significant. Indeed, other schools in the district, where the innovation was tried, reported no change in student achievement after a similar period of implementation. Our conclusion? There are surely teachers like Loretta and Claire in many schools, but distressingly few bring about the notable successes that these two achieved. When the extraordinary nature of their achievements is better understood, when such achievement is named as true leadership and accorded the recognition it deserves, we believe that it will become a contagious force.

Probing the Work of Teacher Leaders: An Exhilarating Endeavor

The material in the two snapshots is both extraordinary and commonplace. Probing the work of teacher leaders is exhilarating in that it reveals aspects of the teaching profession that are largely obscured in the educational literature and in current practice. Several long-held assumptions are challenged in the process. The principals and staff at Greenhills and Sunbeach articulate and model a conviction that public education can provide the best possible opportunities for students, and that factors like isolation and economic disadvantage are no excuse for mediocrity.

The snapshots focus on ways that classroom teachers have brought about significant educational and social change in their schools and communities. The featured teachers involved both their professional and civic communities in the construction of new knowledge that inspired confidence and laid the foundations for heightened aspirations and enhanced levels of student achievement. In effect, the sketches offer a glimpse of the futuristic social transformation advocated by reformists like Drucker (1994) in the United States, Hargreaves (1994) in Canada, and Beare (2001) in Australia. Transformation of this order can occur relatively painlessly when teachers assume the mantle of leadership, and it can be very powerful.

The two snapshots present the work of a small cadre of teachers in a manner that defies the traditional mindset that teachers do not have the capacity, inclination, or opportunity to do leaders' work. The featured teachers displayed conviction, courage, reasonableness, professional knowledge, and a wide range of persuasive and interactive skills. The "I'm just a teacher" syndrome that has come to characterize self-concept in the teaching profession worldwide is far removed from these descriptions.

At the same time, the material in these two snapshots is relatively commonplace. Our research has established that teacher leadership exists in its own right. Katzenmeyer and Moller (1996) provide a powerful picture when they compare teacher leadership to a sleeping giant and assert that where teacher leadership is alive and well, schools flourish. We agree and can see clear signs that the giant is rousing. Will it be a friendly giant? What should we now be doing to prepare for its arrival and ensure its productive impact in our schools and communities?

Here we are clear that the sleeping giant of teacher leadership is indeed rousing, its image discernible, its movement palpable. These developments we regard with enthusiasm but also with a degree of trepidation, because they could dramatically reshape the school workplace, the status of the teaching profession, and the place of schools within communities.

Teachers as Leaders Framework

Our definition of teacher leadership:

> Teacher leadership facilitates principled action to achieve whole-school success. It applies the distinctive power of teaching to shape meaning for children, youth, and adults. And it contributes to long-term, enhanced quality of community life.

The Teachers as Leaders Framework presented in Table 1.1 emphasizes two aspects of this definition: (a) the values of teachers who enhance student outcomes and elevate the quality of life in their schools and communities, and (b) the power of teaching to create new meaning for people in schools and communities.

The framework presents an idealized image of how teacher leaders exercise influence in their school communities. It reflects the essence of the work of teachers designated as leaders in their schools, their communities, and their profession. In a sense, the framework is a hypothetical portrait, because no one teacher leader whom we observed fulfills all six elements. Yet all the teacher leaders whom we studied exhibited aspects of the six elements in some way, at some time in their work. The framework can thus be regarded as both idealized image and pragmatic guide to action.

Many teachers, perhaps most, do not meet the formidable requirements of the definition and the framework in its entirety. In particular, we recognize that consciousness of the power of teaching to shape meaning systems is not well developed in many schools or, indeed, throughout the teaching profession. Some would argue, legitimately in our view, that many educational innovations cause teachers' professional skills to atrophy (Apple, 1992) rather than to enrich their understanding of their marked capabilities.

There are good reasons that some teachers may not seek to link their work to the dynamics of communities in the way our definition prescribes. For example, teachers may choose to pursue subject matter specialization, research, administration, or a range of other challenging occupational avenues that do not necessarily lead to teacher leadership as defined here. Moreover, some teachers who exert leadership at a certain juncture in their careers, or in a particular educational context, may not choose to do so at another time or in another context.

Furthermore, the capabilities required to exercise influence on professional processes of learning and on community agencies are complex. One cannot assume that all teachers have the energy, confidence, or experience to engage influentially at all times. Finally, our research suggests that teacher leadership occurs most readily in supportive organizational environments. But environments that support and nurture teacher leadership are not endemic to many schools.

Despite these drawbacks, there are far more classroom teachers who do meet the demanding requirements of this definition than one might assume. (See Table 1.1 for a portrait of the teacher as leader.) These individuals and collegial groups have, for the most part, been overlooked in the development of leadership theory in recent decades, and have been largely bypassed in the development of policy governing schools. These oversights have cost us all dearly. They have inhibited educational reform and helped to marginalize the teaching profession.

The Framework in Action

The teacher leaders whom we studied, and whose work is captured in the Teachers as Leaders Framework, regarded themselves as ordinary citizens, bound by the usual limitations and imperfections. Yet they were doing what appeared to their colleagues, principals, and communities to be extraordinary things. This combination of the ordinary and the extraordinary is reflected in the connections between the material in the snapshots and the elements of the framework. Teacher leaders have certain characteristics in common—which we will now discuss.

Teacher Leaders Convey Conviction About a Better World

At Greenhills, preparing students for a better future provided the motivation for the teacher leaders. They understood the generally severe disadvantage of students' backgrounds and felt responsible for preparing students for the world of work. Lisa explained it this way: "As teachers, we can help these kids realize that they can do anything that kids in advantaged high schools can do. Getting the confidence is the key step for students in making the break."

At Sunbeach, Claire told us, "My motivation in supporting the literacy program came about because I am committed to getting a better deal for public schools."

Some colleagues saw Claire's stance as provocative, but she did not shy from asserting it publicly. The principal, Paul, reinforced her in subtle ways, emphasizing the complexity of teachers' work: "I personally couldn't do what these teachers do. It is incredible how they take these kids and teach them such extraordinarily complex processes."

Explicit in both of these teaching-and-learning settings is the capacity to create new meaning and new forms of socially useful knowledge. The ability to meet what is, perhaps, the most challenging and, for some, frightening requirement of a knowledge-based society is, therefore, apparent. Teachers are the professionals into whose laps the responsibility most directly falls for helping children realize their talents and opportunities. But that responsibility implies the introduction of new values, new understandings, and new capabilities—a daunting challenge.

Evident at both Greenhills and Sunbeach is leadership that drew on distinctive personal attributes of teachers, leadership grounded in a vision of a positive and optimistic future for disadvantaged students. But it was not personal attributes or vision alone that constituted leadership in these two situations. Rather, leadership, as we observed it, was also exercised through interactive processes that were centered on serious professional and communal dialogue and trust.

Teacher Leaders Strive for Authenticity

At Greenhills, the Student Aspirations Program was, in some respects, an integrating force in the school, linked to all subjects and to extracurricular activities, such as debating, work experience, sports, personal development, and personal mentoring. It was based on educational principles and on teachers' perceptions of students' needs to take responsibility for their own learning, to study relevant content, and constantly to expand their view of the world. What emerged was distinctive to the school: As one teacher noted, "Once you become a part of Aspirations, you are a changed person as well as a changed teacher. The way you interact and engage is different from what it would be anywhere else."

At Sunbeach, Loretta recognized that to be effective, the literacy program had to be a schoolwide initiative. She emphasized the integration of the program into regular classroom literacy activities and coordinated it with parent literacy initiatives. The question "Will it work for *all* of our kids?" was a focus of staff dialogue during this trial period. Ultimately, Loretta's insight and conviction influenced other teachers' approach to literacy.

Authenticity in teaching, learning, and assessment practices took on a number of meanings in our snapshot studies: shared understanding of learning goals across the school; learning goals grounded in students' needs and evident in teachers' practice; an integration of teaching, learning, and assessment; and actions justified by authoritative educational theory. This is an imposing set of criteria, in part because it extends the boundaries of classroom instruction in a number of directions—engaging the broader community in shared learning, the creation of new forms of pedagogy, and the extension of academic ideas into community action.

Teacher Leaders Facilitate Communities of Learning

At Greenhills, community apathy toward the school turned into expansive support once successes became evident. The teacher leaders themselves derived strength and confidence from one another. In fact, the informal alliance of teachers and administrators working as equal partners proved to be the root of the school's success. From this highly visible and successful alliance, community agencies were easily linked into Aspirations and other school programs.

At Sunbeach, too, an informal professional group (a teacher, a learning-support teacher, and the principal) initiated a highly successful innovation. Elementary teachers were the first formal group to be integrated into this collegial network. It was further expanded in response to the expressed interest of individual teachers, following staff discussions on the merits of the program. This program was also extended to include a cluster of nearby schools.

Rosabeth Kanter (1994) wrote that "like romances, the formation of alliances rests largely on hopes and dreams—what might be possible if certain opportunities are pursued" (p. 95). The teacher leaders we observed demonstrated practical capacity to build alliances and networks in many forms, thereby engendering the creation of new ideas, dreams, and opportunities that would not otherwise have existed.

Teacher Leaders Confront Barriers

When Lisa approached the Greenhills principal to ask for one more chance for a highly disruptive student who was threatened with exclusion, she epitomized the social-justice orientation of Greenhills teacher leaders and their preparedness to extend ideals into social action. This orientation included a wide range of activities, including provision of basic food and laundry services for needy students. The principal summed up the advocacy role of teacher leaders as follows: "I regard the teachers here as the guardians of the culture. They take personal responsibility for managing projects that fit the school's vision."

At Sunbeach, Claire located two significant funding sources to support the innovative literacy program, and coordinated the grant application process. Her colleague, Loretta, who had conceived the literacy project, generated an extensive training program for the staff and organized the planning that led to a smoothly running operation. Loretta's capacity for social action was apparent in her statement that even without the facilitative support of the principal, "I would do it in some form myself."

These examples capture the essence of teaching against the grain that some theorists have articulated in projecting images of teacher leadership. They manifest conviction, courage, and strategic skill that might not be expected of most teachers and, thus, might be generally discouraged. They are, however, essential to teacher leadership and to the pursuit of enhanced schooling and quality of life in our communities.

Teacher Leaders Translate Ideas Into Action

At both Greenhills and Sunbeach, the teacher leaders whom we observed articulated deep concerns regarding the sustainability of the innovations with which they were associated. In both instances, they translated their concern into direct actions that contributed to the ongoing implementation of their innovations. Thus at Sunbeach, Loretta mobilized staff development processes, with the support of a deputy principal, and also engineered a range of highly successful community awareness programs. At Greenhills, teachers managed all aspects of the Aspirations program, including curriculum, community service, publicity, and budget. In creating and sustaining productive relationships with school administrators and with external constituencies, and in using the Aspirations program to enrich the self-perceptions of a severely disadvantaged community, these teachers could be said to have entered the arena of metastrategy that we draw on in Chapter 4 and that Limerick, Cunnington, and Crowther (1998) regard as fundamental to leadership in postindustrial organizations.

Teacher Leaders Nurture a Culture of Success

At Greenhills, the teacher leaders collectively emphasized a "we can do anything" attitude. This had a demonstrable impact on students' self-esteem and achievement. Even seemingly insignificant achievements were held up as evidence that all students can achieve beyond normal expectations when they are encouraged and recognized. The Greenhills principal provided us bemusedly with this example: "Even a student taking a cow to the Blackbutt Fair can provide a basis for building confidence. These shows bore me silly except for what I can do for the school just by being there."

Successes of past students in the outside world were also offered regularly as evidence that success breeds success and that small achievements can turn into bigger ones, once a start is made.

At Sunbeach, Loretta's infectious optimism energized others. The school's successes in the national Innovation and Best Practice Project (IBPP) were presented as proof that it is quite realistic to articulate and pursue lofty expectations. When Loretta and Claire prematurely terminated an IBPP research contract, they did so in the confident spirit of Sunbeach: "People are not to blame for failing to achieve high expectations. It is more likely the processes *we* [emphasis added] have in place that are flawed." Amid the disillusionment and anxiety that creeps into our lives, success may be hard to recognize and equally hard for many of us to acknowledge. But leaders routinely recognize and acknowledge success. Teacher leaders do so to enhance confidence, induce high expectations, and extend horizons for their students. In the process, the uncertainty of the emerging knowledge-based society becomes not a threat but a promise for a better future.

Conclusions

In this chapter, we have presented a definition of teacher leadership and a related framework that derives from extensive research in diverse school settings. We regard this definition and framework as confirmation of a capacity for professional leadership that has been obscured in the literature on educational leadership and in most professional development programs for practicing and aspiring educational leaders.

In the eyes of their colleagues, principals, and communities, the teacher leaders whom we studied have a remarkable impact on their schools and communities. The Teachers as Leaders Framework captures these ordinary people doing extraordinary things. Their leadership is well suited to a postindustrial world where hierarchy in organizational relationships will decrease in importance, and the capacity to help communities enhance their quality of life through the creation of knowledge will increase.

CHAPTER 2

Five Premises to Guide Revitalization of the Teaching Profession

Teacher leadership is not a new concept. As is so often the case in the field of education, however, we continue to struggle with basic definitions of terms which should be inherent in our professional vocabulary

— Eloise Forster (1997, p. 82)

Meeting the Current Challenge

The Teachers as Leaders Framework (Table 1.1) represents, in our view, a plausible response to the point raised above by Forster. It also provides the clear and meaningful performance criteria that must be available to the teaching profession if it is to become a leading profession, perhaps the leading profession, in the years ahead. The framework makes apparent what teacher leadership looks like and what differentiates it from other forms of teacher professionalism, including specialist expertise in a variety of areas.

There are, however, no guarantees that Katzenmeyer and Moller's (1996) sleeping giant will rouse just because there is a need for it to or because we think it should. One cannot take for granted that teacher leadership will, through natural evolutionary processes, become ingrained in our collective consciousness and thus realize its potential. To the contrary, the challenge confronting the education community in further exploring the meaning of teacher leadership and ensuring its applications in schools is massive. The importance of accepting this challenge is, of course, equally great.

Where, then, to start?

In this chapter, we propose five premises that we believe are supportable on the basis of our own and related international research and that, viewed together, constitute a compelling rationale for a new professionalism for teachers worldwide. Our contention is that teacher leadership exists as an entity in its own right. As this idea becomes widespread, the implications for school reform, and for the role of the teaching profession in a knowledge-based society, will be profound.

Before discussing these five critical premises, it may be helpful to reflect on another case study in which the well-being of a school and its community was positively affected by teachers' work in generating new knowledge.

A Snapshot

Snapshot: Bordertown State High School

Bordertown has 400 students and is situated in a relatively remote rural town built around the cotton industry. Recent school-administered surveys yielded findings that were devastating to many of its teachers, but not unexpected to outside observers. Staff morale was assessed as low, the community's perceptions of the school were overwhelmingly negative, and student achievement was largely regarded as unsatisfactory. Could a positive future be created out of such a negative scenario? Perhaps not, but the deputy principal and a team of volunteer teachers who formed a school revitalization team felt they had to make a concerted effort.

The school's location in a medium-sized town at the center of a thriving cotton-growing community did not make the task any easier. Community leaders had a reputation for entrepreneurship and assertiveness (as well as parochialism) and viewed the school's achievements as inadequate compared to their own achievements in the corporate world. Academically inclined students frequently left home to attend expensive private schools, contributing further to the school's second-class image.

But within 2 years of the administration of the surveys, the school had become a State Showcase Award winner, nationally known for its Bordertown Pedagogical Framework. (Bordertown is in Australia, where *pedagogical* has a meaning different from its meaning in American English; in Australia, the word denotes the function, work, and art of a teacher; in American English, it denotes relating to education or to a teacher.) Teacher morale had increased dramatically, the school was a key source of community pride, and links with the cotton industry for vocational training programs were formalized. Additionally, some students attending private schools returned to the local high school, and aspects of student achievement schoolwide improved noticeably.

Three leadership dimensions underpinned the revitalization process at Bordertown—a dynamic, ambitious deputy principal who, in essence, assumed the role of principal because the actual principal was near retirement; a supportive facilitator and important friend from a nearby university; and a core team of five teachers, two of whom were part-time department heads (a third was a beginning teacher, and two more had married into the local community and expected to stay).

The revitalization process proceeded on a number of interlocking fronts—revisioning, community building, creating and trying out new educational practices in a range of years and subjects, and concerted professional and public promotion of the school. Teacher leaders were integral to each of these processes, but particularly to the generation of the school's pedagogical framework that is described in Table 2.1. Three comments from participants in the process, following two years of exceptionally successful revitalization, offer perspective on Bordertown's success:

> "The opportunities we've had have liberated us. In creating ideas that we would never have imagined to be possible, we have become different people."

> "We have learned to listen to each other, talk to each other, learn from each other, all because we have come to believe that as teachers, we are real leaders who can create new ideas. We know how to move mountains."

> "I love coming to council meetings. It's so refreshing to see creativity and ideas in action." (School Council Chair)

Revitalizing the Teaching Profession From Within

Case studies such as Greenhills and Sunbeach (Chapter 1) and Bordertown (this chapter) stand as testimony that where successful school reform is in place, teachers play essential leader roles. Their leadership

Table 2.1 Bordertown State High School's Educational Framework

Together we achieve
- The creation of lifelong learners
- An enriched community
- Flexible pathways to the future

Our definition of schoolwide pedagogy is
- Self-awareness
  What does this experience tell me about myself?
- Critical reflection
  Why am I doing this?
- Personal development
  How has this contributed to my development?
- Communication
  How could I demonstrate what I know?
- Cooperation
  How does this experience enable us to learn from each other?
- Application
  How can this be applied now or later?
- An enriched community
  How does this enrich our school community?
- Future direction
  What will this be like in the future?

Source: Closely based on the Schoolwide Pedagogical Framework created by Goondiwindi High School, Queensland, Australia. Used with permission.

work is centered on their own professional practice (but extends to schoolwide teaching, learning, and assessment practices), as well as on community dynamics. Thus teacher leaders exercise influence well beyond their individual classrooms. They demonstrate how knowledge is created and what new knowledge looks like. They are, as may be inferred from the statement by Drucker (1994) with which we opened the preface to this book, core knowledge workers, who will give the emerging knowledge society its character, its leadership, and its social profile.

In Bordertown, it was the school's framework for teaching and learning that particularly captivated the interest of the local business community. As one teacher explained to us:

Only a school could develop a model like this [teaching-and-learning framework]. For all sorts of reasons, churches can't do it, clubs can't do it, commercial agencies can't do it, and town councils can't do it. Teachers working like this can shape people's thoughts and values into concepts. When they do that, they give the whole town new understandings about itself, something to identify with.

Five Premises to Guide the Development of the Profession

Based on our research and on the associated work of Conley and Muncey (1999), Darling-Hammond (1997), Forster (1997), Katzenmeyer and Moller (1996), King and Newmann (1999), and Louis, Marks and Kruse (1996), among others, we confidently advance five premises to guide the teaching profession and the general education community, as the postindustrial era unfolds. We present these premises for the consideration of educators who function in a range of professional venues—professional development agencies, policy development forums, preservice teacher education programs, and principals' development and certification processes.

> Premise One: Teacher leadership exists; it is real.
>
> Premise Two: Teacher leadership is grounded in authoritative theory.
>
> Premise Three: Teacher leadership is distinctive.
>
> Premise Four: Teacher leadership is diverse.
>
> Premise Five: Teacher leadership can be nurtured.

Premise One: Teacher Leadership Exists; It Is Real

Teacher leadership is more than a promising concept with potential for future positive effects. It is observable in schools now, and it can be described in clear terms. By any standards for judging, teacher leadership exists. It is real.

The Teachers as Leaders Framework is based on the work of classroom teachers who compelled attention because of their powerful ideas-in-action. As researchers, we documented these actions, described and analyzed their dynamics, and translated them into concepts that made sense to the teachers, their colleagues, and their principals.

Thus the framework captures, in generalized form, the essence of the professional lives of many classroom teachers at particular junctures. Situations we observed and documented varied from largely individual ideas-in-action to mainly collective ideas-in-action. At Bordertown, for example, a small group of teacher leaders and their deputy principal confronted, head-on, school and community disillusionment and apathy. In a short time, the school became a dynamic source of pride for the community. The six elements of the Teachers as Leaders Framework were all readily identifiable in the work of these professionals, individually and collectively, as they are in the two snapshots in Chapter 1.

The notion that teaching will evolve into a leading profession depends on teacher leadership in schools. Without evidence of teachers as leaders, there is little prospect of the creation of the new paradigm for the teaching profession called for by people like Darling-Hammond (1997) and Hargreaves (1994). Nor is there much prospect for the creation of a dynamic new form of professionalism, such as that proposed by Judyth Sachs (as cited in Day, 2000), who has identified five core values that constitute the fundamentals of an active, responsible approach to teacher professionalism:

- **Learning,** in which teachers are seen to practice learning, individually and with their colleagues and students

- **Participation,** in which teachers see themselves as active agents in their own professional worlds

- **Collaboration,** in which collegiality is exercised within and between internal and external communities

- **Cooperation,** through which teachers develop a common language and technology for documenting and discussing practice and desired outcomes (pp. 84-85)

- **Activism,** in which teachers "engage publicly with issues that relate directly or indirectly to education and schooling as part of their moral purposes." (p. 115)

The teacher leaders at Bordertown High met all five of Sachs's criteria in developing the Bordertown Schoolwide Pedagogical Framework and in applying it to school and community developmental processes. Based on case studies such as this, our research leads us to conclude that Sachs's vision for the teaching profession is eminently realistic. Of course, much work remains to be done before teacher leadership takes root as a compelling, pervasive movement.

Premise Two: Teacher Leadership Is Grounded in Authoritative Theory

In our search for a new professionalism for teachers—one that honors teaching as a profession and teachers' work as fundamental in postindustrial learning communities—we investigated the literature on educational leadership. We found a striking lack of recognition of teachers as either potential or actual leaders in schools. Thus the question of whether the accepted body of thought on educational leadership is an asset or a liability to efforts at formulating a concept of teacher leadership is an important one—and one that does not appear, on the surface, to engender optimism.

A quick look at the history of educational leadership theory reveals just why past concepts offer little support for new forms of leadership. Educational leadership is firmly grounded in ideas about authority that stem from Weber's notion of legitimate power (Mayer, 1943). Weber, with his focus on hierarchical coordination in bureaucracies, noted that authority constituted the right to command, to instruct, to order, and to exercise sanctions in support of such commands. To early management theorists, the role of prescribed authority was basic. Pioneer theorists like Katz and Kahn (1966), for example, observed that "the management sub-system in every organization and the structure of authority are inseparable" (p. 203). In other words, a structure of official persons who have the right to command is essential to conditions of order, coordinated effort, and goal attainment.

A number of classic, educational, administration texts have, not surprisingly, followed this line of thinking. Hoy and Miskel (1991) provide the following advice to students enrolled in postgraduate courses in educational administration: "When teachers join a school organization, they accept the formal authority relation. They agree within certain limits to follow directives that administrators issue. In short, they enter into contractual agreements in which they sell their promises to obey commands" (p. 78).

Bates (1983) summed up this ideological perspective on educational administration, and his perception of its immense impact on contemporary practice, when he stated, "Educational administration is a technology of control. . . . The concepts, the theories, and the organizing systems are a clear indication of a preoccupation with control that is endemic to the occupation" (p. 8).

Under the influence of theorists like Bates, the relationship between authority and leadership has come to be regarded, during the past two decades, as problematic. Nevertheless, both educational policy and leadership theory continue to operate, for the most part, on the flawed rationale that equates position with leadership. Regarding policy, it is not surprising that significant American initiatives of the past 2 decades to formalize teacher leadership, such as master teacher and merit pay schemes, have enjoyed relatively limited success or sustainability (Leithwood & Jantzi, 1998; Ponder & Holmes, 2000). In Australia, the Advanced Skill Teacher Reforms of the early 1990s have been similarly documented as "a disappointment and an opportunity lost" (Ingvarson & Chadbourne, 1996, p. 59).

We conclude from our analysis of international research that what may appear as an easy solution to a complex issue—motivating teachers to move their colleagues toward externally determined and directed purposes through the provision of concrete rewards—simply does not work well in a mature profession such as teaching.

Regarding theories of leadership, consider four well-known approaches to contemporary educational leadership and the place that teacher leadership occupies in each. We discuss them briefly here as transformational, strategic, educative, and organizational.

Transformational leadership emphasizes the significance of the person and personal traits in bringing about social and cultural change. To Avolio and Bass (1988), whose pioneering research was instrumental in developing transformational approaches to leadership, leaders are individuals who "motivate followers to work for transcendental goals instead of immediate self-interest, and for achievement and self-actualization instead of safety and security" (p. 33). Transformational leadership, with its associated concepts of charisma and inspiration, has frequently been proposed as the most appropriate leadership approach for school principals and as the prerogative of principals (Leithwood, 1994). Consistent with this line of thinking is a recent British study by Day (2000, p. 117) that concluded that effective principals are transformative and that they require the ability to engage reflectively in a much more complex, broader range of contexts than do teachers. Little space appears, for the most part, to have been allowed in the transformational approach for significant teacher leadership.

Strategic leadership, as the term clearly implies, emphasizes systematic, rational management in leaders' roles. Hambrick (1989) suggests that it involves aligning the organization with anticipated external forces—technological developments, market trends, regulatory constraints, competitors' actions, and so on. Like Hambrick, Caldwell (1992) has advocated a leadership function that is primarily strategic as the most appropriate approach for principals in self-managing schools:

> The principal must be able to develop and implement a cyclical process of goal-setting, need identification, priority setting, policy making, planning, budgeting, implementing and evaluating in a manner which provides for the appropriate involvement of staff and community, including parents and students as relevant. The complexity of the process in respect to the numbers of actors indicates a capacity to manage conflict. (pp. 16-17)

Strategic processes such as those identified by Caldwell are undoubtedly relevant to the work of school principals. But what meaning, if any, do they have in the work of highly successful classroom teachers and other non-administrators? This question has received little serious consideration in the literature on educational leadership.

Educative leadership is generally viewed as linked to organizational reculturing, a process that cannot be removed from teachers' work. Duignan and Macpherson (1992) define it as follows:

> Educative leadership . . . must closely respond to the cultural context, be critically aware of the long-term practices of participants in educational processes, and when action is proposed, justify ends and processes using an educative philosophy . . . Hence, educative leadership implies a responsible involvement in the politics of organization. (pp. 3-4)

Bates (1992) affirms the importance of educational leadership as culture building when he says that it "involves the making and articulating of choices, the location of oneself within the cultural struggles of the times as much in the cultural battles of the school as in the wider society" (p. 19). Implicit in Bates's challenge is the view that, if education is to create human emancipation or liberation, it will be unlikely to do so through the sole influence of administrators. Still, some authorities have noted that, although educational leadership is not tied to position, it is the school principal who has most opportunity to exercise leadership of this type (Rizvi, 1992, pp. 137, 163). The potential of educational concepts and processes to explain the work of teachers as leaders within the context of the school community remains relatively unexplored.

Leadership as an organizational quality is a recent concept that seems, on the surface, to be consistent with the notion of teachers as leaders. We say this because it implies the existence of leadership capabilities throughout organizations, including schools, and centers attention on core organizational processes rather than on individuals. Both conditions appear to be consistent with the work of teachers, especially as schools enter a knowledge society in which processes of learning are paramount. Pounder, Ogawa, and Adams (1995) explain this approach to leadership in schools:

> The concept of leadership as an organizational quality suggests that the total amount of leadership found in schools will have a positive relationship to their performance. Furthermore, it suggests that all members of schools—including principals, teachers, staff members, and parents—can lead and thus affect the performance of their schools. (p. 567)

Similar notions regarding leadership as a shared responsibility are articulated in recent literature and include multiple-role leadership (Limerick, Cunnington, & Crowther, 1998), distributed leadership (Handy, 1996), leadership of the many (Lakomski, 1995), collective intelligence (Heifetz & Laurie, 1997), community of leaders (Senge, 1997), and co-leadership (Heenan & Bennis, 1999). Concepts like these—recognizing, as they do, that today's leaders can come from many places and assume many forms—are increasingly significant in management and organizational literature.

Significantly, however, leadership theories grounded in shared responsibility often tend to reify the role of formal authority in the same way as more traditional theories. Thus Heenan and Bennis's (1999) concept of co-leadership is presented as a relationship between chief executives and their immediate subordinates; and Heifetz and Laurie (1997), in emphasizing the importance of "collective intelligence," nevertheless, speak of "a leader" and "senior managers" (p. 127).

Taken together, these four approaches to leadership greatly enrich our understanding of school-based leadership, but they have not been explored systematically in conjunction with processes of successful school revitalization. It appears that what Hallinger and Heck (1996) described as the black box of school leadership continues for the most part to pervade research and theory: "The process by which administrators achieve an impact is hidden in a so-called black box. A relationship is empirically tested, but the findings reveal little about how leadership operates" (p. 8).

Most important, none of the four leadership approaches that we have described has been developed or explored seriously with an eye to the possible leadership roles of teachers. None conceptualizes leadership in relation to teachers' core functions, and none appears to take into account the maturity and sophistication that characterizes contemporary teaching. Just as a new paradigm of the teaching profession is warranted, so, too, is a new paradigm of leadership—one that recognizes the central place of teachers. In sum, current educational leadership theories appear to be at least as much a liability as an asset for the task we have set ourselves.

Two promising developments are, nevertheless, taking hold. The first is an expressed need, within all organizations including schools, for enhanced relationships between formal leaders—directors of organizational units—and so-called followers, some of whom may be de facto leaders. In leadership of this type, supervisor and supervisee distribute between them the authority and responsibility for a given organizational task. John Nirenberg's (1993) *The Living Organization* highlights this idea and then takes it a step further:

> It is not leadership from any one person that is required, it is an aspect of leadership each of us summons from within. In this respect the same qualities we have sought in one person can be found distributed among many people who learn, in community, to exercise their leadership at appropriate moments. This occurs when people are vitally concerned about issues or when executing their responsibilities. Leadership thus becomes a rather fluid concept focusing on those behaviors that propel the work of the group forward. (p. 198)

This observation highlights the idea of leadership as relatedness. In so doing, it expands on the variations of shared leadership that we have outlined above and focuses on what can happen between people through participation, partnership, and service.

Another significant recent development has to do with recognition of the importance of culture as a leadership domain. The authoritative scholarship of Schein (1992, p. 2) in linking leadership with cultural creation has been extended into change management processes by a number of scholars, including, for example, Hargreaves (1994), who has asserted that "Culture carries the community's historically generated and collectively shared solutions to its new and inexperienced membership. It forms a framework for occupational learning" (p. 165). Similarly, Senge (2000) has recently described the professional community of the school as "the container that holds the culture" (p. 326), implying that culture building and the collective work of teachers are inseparable. The integration of leadership and culture building is particularly prominent in Catholic education where, for example, faith is seen as inseparable from life (Abbott, 1966), and the Catholic school is seen as increasingly responsible for transmitting the Christian message (Congregation of Catholic Education, 1998; Flynn, 1979).

We find it extremely significant that all the leadership theories we reviewed included factors that are evident in the work of the teacher leaders whom we studied. For example, teacher leaders develop and execute complex strategies; they engage in management activities; and they design and negotiate plans across levels, systems, discipline areas, and governance bodies. In effect, our studies reveal that elements of strategic leadership, although historically regarded as the preserve of administrators, particularly principals is, in fact, apparent in the work of teacher leaders.

Concrete evidence of transformational leadership also appeared in the work of teachers in all the reforms we studied. In fact, our research shows that reform is most easily achieved when principals demonstrate conviction and passion about an organizational vision, and teacher leaders demonstrate complementary educational values and aspirations. For successful reform to occur, congruence in the visions of principals and teacher leaders is, in fact, paramount.

Educational reform was a prominent feature of the work of teacher leaders in all our case studies. It was frequently tied to a deep-rooted concern for the disadvantaged, for social justice, or for marginalization. And it was tied to a need to confront political barriers and to raise professional and community consciousness. Perhaps because advocacy is difficult for many principals in workplaces dominated by political agendas, in most of our studies, educational leadership was more apparent in the work of teachers than of administrators. Yet their principals appreciated teachers' successful innovations and supported the strong values of teacher leaders, even when the principals did not fully share those values.

Finally, emerging leadership theories that emphasize shared responsibility and interconnection were well represented in the work of teacher leaders we studied. Perhaps most critically, our case studies make clear that the creation of new knowledge and meaning in schools and their communities is dependent, in large part, on teachers' leadership in generating and applying schoolwide educational reform. In addition to providing clear links with well-established leadership theories, the Teachers as Leaders Framework is consistent with the concept of emotional intelligence that Goleman (1998) asserts is the "sine qua non for leadership" (p. 93). This is evident in Figure 2.1, in the matching of Goleman's four components of emotional intelligence with the six elements of the framework.

We conclude Premise Two by asserting that the traditional tendency to associate leadership with formal authority will probably inhibit sustained school reform in the years ahead because it fails to take advantage of those leaders who are most closely associated with the central function of schools—namely, classroom teachers. A concept of school leadership that recognizes that at least some classroom teachers possess the full range of leadership capabilities described in authoritative theories is essential for successful school reform in a knowledge-based society.

Premise Three: Teacher Leadership Is Distinctive

Central to our framework, as we have noted, is the capacity of teachers to generate authentic approaches to teaching, learning, and assessment (Newmann & Wehlage, 1995). Essential to such development is schoolwide understanding of the diversity of teaching approaches within a school (Crowther, Andrews, Dawson, & Lewis, 2001; Crowther, Hann, & McMaster, 2001; King & Newmann, 2000; Newmann & Wehlage, 1995). Appreciating this diversity requires illumination of teachers' philosophies, dreams, and aspirations. It also requires identifying the common ground of teachers' classroom successes across subject areas, teaching levels, age, experience, and gender.

It is unlikely that administrators or external consultants, however capable, can manage the complex and sensitive development of schoolwide approaches to teaching and learning without teacher leadership. In our case studies, these processes were engaged, with positive results for students and school communities. In all instances, practicing teachers fulfilled complex, subtle, and responsible roles in schoolwide pedagogical development that are not reflected in leadership theories derived from the field of educational administration.

Teacher leadership is essential to school success based on collective purpose and effort. Coherence and consistency in a school's educational philosophy make it easier to develop depth and authenticity in individual teaching; and professional relevance is key to synergistic school development. Put simply, teacher leadership is grounded in the philosophy that, in schools that achieve their potential, the whole is greater than the sum of the parts. In one of our case study schools, the motto, "A champion team will always beat a team of champions," was

Figure 2.1. Linking the Teachers as Leaders Framework With Goleman's Emotional Intelligence

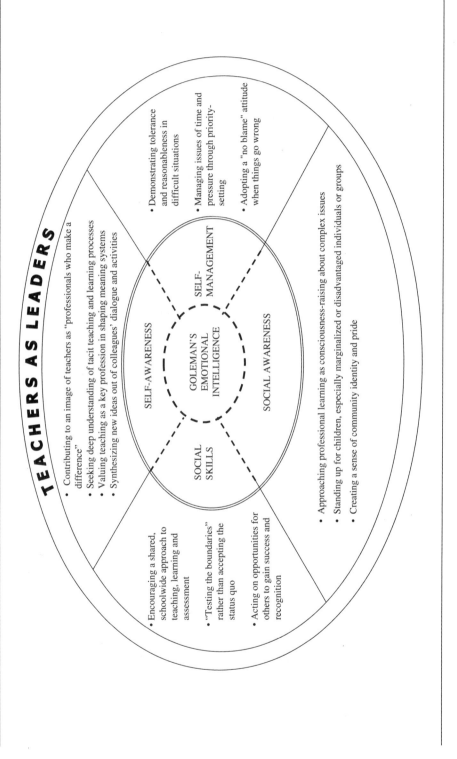

TEACHERS AS LEADERS

GOLEMAN'S EMOTIONAL INTELLIGENCE

SELF-AWARENESS
- Contributing to an image of teachers as "professionals who make a difference"
- Seeking deep understanding of tacit teaching and learning processes
- Valuing teaching as a key profession in shaping meaning systems
- Synthesizing new ideas out of colleagues' dialogue and activities

SELF-MANAGEMENT
- Demonstrating tolerance and reasonableness in difficult situations
- Managing issues of time and pressure through priority-setting
- Adopting a "no blame" attitude when things go wrong

SOCIAL SKILLS
- Encouraging a shared, schoolwide approach to teaching, learning and assessment
- "Testing the boundaries" rather than accepting the status quo
- Acting on opportunities for others to gain success and recognition

SOCIAL AWARENESS
- Approaching professional learning as consciousness-raising about complex issues
- Standing up for children, especially marginalized or disadvantaged individuals or groups
- Creating a sense of community identity and pride

used by teacher leaders and their principal. The motto was a reminder that schools do not achieve their potential until their elements are fully aligned: vision; teaching, learning and assessment practices; use of time, space, and technologies; community values; and teachers' professional development. Without teacher leadership, of course, such alignment can rarely, if ever, happen.

It is primarily through teacher leadership that schools generate new meaning and, in so doing, enhance their community's quality of life. Schoolwide approaches to teaching, learning, and assessment can develop new meaning—new or enriched forms of school identity and culture. Therefore we assert that teacher leadership is a distinctive form of leadership, and teachers are particularly well placed to assume leadership in a world where knowledge generation will be fundamental to community and global sustainability.

Premise Four: Teacher Leadership Is Diverse

Teacher leaders may be found in both advantaged and disadvantaged schools, in denominational, private, and public schools, at all grade and year levels, and across all subjects and disciplines. They reflect a wide range of dispositions, political allegiances, religious affiliations, personalities, ages, and other characteristics. Teacher leaders as individuals may prefer classical, technological, or humanistic approaches to teaching and learning. Any attempt to identify teacher leaders in advance of observing them in context has been, in our experience, unsuccessful. Teacher leadership is characterized by remarkable diversity and, in that diversity, resides complexity.

We tend to resist the popular view that teacher leadership can be defined by identifiable personal or professional attributes. But Leithwood, Jantzi, Ryan, and Steinbach (1997) propose a revealing profile of teacher leadership:

> The composite teacher leader is warm, dependable, and self-effacing with a genuine commitment to the work of colleagues and the school. She has well-honed interpersonal skills which are exercised with individuals and groups of colleagues, as well as with students. In addition, the teacher leader possesses the technical skills required for program improvement and uses them in concert with a broad knowledge base about education policy, subject matter, the local community and the school's students. (pp. 23–24)

Although attempts such as this to conceptualize teacher leadership highlight the human dimension of school-based leadership, they can be criticized on the same grounds that behavioral and trait approaches to leadership have been criticized for many years—they deny the capabilities of individuals whose characteristics and talents lie in areas other than those identified. It could also be said that they deny that ordinary mortals can assume leadership.

Teacher leadership is powerful in its diversity, its sensitivity to situation and context, and its capacity to enhance and enrich communal meaning and quality of life. Without exception, the teacher leaders we observed showed deep regard for their communities' values while, at the same time, striving to establish links between their students' current and future lives. Teacher leadership in communities beset by violence, apathy, and disillusionment is quite different from teacher leadership in schools with a large proportion of students privileged materialistically, culturally, and socially. In the former, teacher leadership may involve action to uplift students' capacity to engage confidently with the broader world. In the latter, it may entail sensitizing students to critical problems confronting the world and encouraging them to accept responsibility for addressing them. In both instances, barriers invariably have to be confronted, trust established, networks created, and successes celebrated. How these actions are approached and undertaken might be very different in different situations.

Are all teachers leaders? Can they be? Should they be? We believe that all teachers are potential leaders, but to suggest that all teachers *are* leaders defies considerations of context, power relations, personal characteristics, and human nature. We have no doubt that, as further defensible formulations of teacher leadership are generated and begin to affect school practice, teacher leadership will expand. And then the capacity of the teaching profession to lead communities forward will be further revealed.

Premise Five: Teacher Leadership Can Be Nurtured

The question of how to develop leadership capabilities is one that has preoccupied theorists and practitioners for decades. What knowledge is basic to leader development? Should leader development be undertaken through mentoring and counseling, through formal training and certification, or perhaps through on-site experience? Should it be based on a prescribed curriculum or on situational and contextual issues? Should potential leaders be identified, in advance, for development, and, if so, what criteria apply in identifying them? These questions represent prominent concerns for educational administrators, particularly for the principal. They are also relevant as we elaborate the concept of teacher leadership and seek to develop leadership within the teaching profession.

Four Conditions for Teacher Leadership

Our case studies, in all instances, featured the emergence and maturation of teacher leadership. Our analyses of the experiences of the teacher leaders lead us to propose that teacher leadership development requires four conditions.

The first condition is public and professional acceptance of the existence of teacher leaders in the profession and in the schools. Our Teachers as Leaders Framework represents a start in responding to this requirement. The successes of teachers whose capacities mirror those in the framework must be celebrated, and their work must be studied and documented.

The second condition is active support of principals and system administrators. At one workshop that we conducted with principals, the focus was on barriers to teacher leadership. A summary of identified barriers and ways to overcome them, suggested by participants in that exercise, are summarized in Table 2.2. In the workshop, some principals expressed enthusiasm for nurturing teacher leadership in their schools. Others, however, were less than enthusiastic about the challenge.

Where we have seen teacher leadership begin to flourish, principals have actively supported it or, at least, encouraged it. Systemwide policies in these schools have also supported teacher leaders, and external mentors have provided encouragement and helped to clarify teacher leader and administrator leader roles. We believe that it is possible for teacher leadership to exist without the support of administrators. But its outcomes will not be as positive as when such leadership is accepted and encouraged. The dynamics of the relationship between teacher leaders and administrator leaders in schools that have achieved successful reforms are examined in Chapters 3 and 4.

The third condition for nurturing teacher leadership is greater development of teachers' roles in school reform and revitalization. We have undertaken to respond to this challenge in Part Two of this book. The 14 exercises that we developed can be undertaken at the initiation either of teachers who aspire to become leaders, or of administrators who wish to nurture teacher leadership in their schools, or both. The exercises encompass a range of consciousness-raising, skill develop-

Table 2.2 Overcoming Barriers to Teacher Leadership

Barriers to Leadership	Ways to Overcome the Barriers
"I'm just a teacher" mindset	Encourage and reward potential teacher leaders (TLs).
Lack of confidence	Step back and give others a chance.
Unclear understanding of the concept	Encourage mentoring from TL models.
"I just want to teach" mindset	Build networks of TLs.
No time for development	Prove TLs make a difference.
System that expects only principals to be leaders	Give teachers *real* responsibilities.
Might encourage rabble rousers	Identify issues where teachers can lead.
Belief that too many cooks spoil the broth	Encourage personal development in the workplace.
No rewards for extra effort	Create time for professional dialogue.
Open to abuse by manipulators	Create clear definitions of TL.
Previous failures with lead teachers	Dispel *authority* = *leadership* notions.
Language that reinforces teachers as subordinates ("bosses"and "staff")	
Not taught in preservice education	
Peer pressure	
Lack of principal support	

ment, and concept-forming activities relating to teacher leadership and parallel leadership—the two central concepts of this book.

The fourth condition for nurturing teacher leadership is the acknowledgement that teacher leadership produces positive school outcomes. Although not enough is known at present about the dynamics through which teacher leadership influences schools, research supports optimism (Crowther, Hann, & McMaster, 2001). The quality of relationships between teacher leaders and administrator leaders, and the interaction among three interrelated processes—professional learning, schoolwide pedagogy, and culture building—appear to be central factors in solidifying the case for linking leadership and positive school improvement.

But some observers assert that an emphasis on teacher leadership may, in fact, deter excellence in teachers' practices. Two particular concerns are cited in education literature. First is the contention that most teachers do not wish to lead, on grounds that it will interfere with their teaching (Leithwood & Jantzi, 1998). Certainly, the view that is expressed as "I just want to teach, I don't want to be a leader" is one that we have heard frequently. Also relevant is Little's (1995) claim that the evolution of teacher leadership in high schools has been accompanied by the emergence of new professional tensions over contested ground. Little applies the concept of contested ground to traditions of subject specialization and their influence on leadership among secondary school teachers.

The claims of observers such as Leithwood and Little do apply to industrial-era schools, but we believe that they are much less applicable today. It is the responsibility of principals and system administrators to ensure that such concerns are taken seriously at the same time that teacher leadership is nurtured.

Conclusions

Teacher leadership is real, it is grounded in authoritative theory, it is distinctive, it is diverse, and it can be nurtured. As these realizations become widespread, the implications for school reform and for the role of teachers will be profound.

Teacher leadership can and, therefore, must be encouraged. We agree with Bolman and Deal (1994) that "leadership can be taught—but not the way we currently do it" (p. 94). Sherrill's (1999) claim that teacher leadership cannot be nurtured without new working relationships between teachers and administrators is also one that we endorse, as we do Kaagan's (1999) assertion that leader development is most effectively undertaken when reflection-in-action is employed as the means to formulate new mental constructs (p. 13). Kaagan's constructivist approach is fundamental to the exercises in Chapter 6.

The five premises in this chapter are a guide to a new professionalism for teachers—a professionalism that is both inspiring in its promise and realistic in its potential.

CHAPTER 3

Parallelism

Building School Capacity Through Shared Leadership

> *Simply put, new and different working relationships need to be established between teachers and administrators in order for any new leadership role to make a positive and lasting contribution to the improvement of teaching and learning in a given setting.*
>
> — Patricia Wasley (as cited in Sherrill, 1999, p. 57)

A Snapshot

Snapshot: West Town High School

West Town High School serves approximately 1,500 students and is located in a provincial city that is endowed with excellent public, private, and sectarian schools serving not only the local community but also a wide surrounding region. For many years, West Town's place in this context was that of a relatively marginalized school without social or economic status. We visited the school at a time when its profile and status had, however, undergone a remarkable transformation, with enrollments bulging (increasing from 750 to 1,450 in a 5-year period) at the expense of neighboring schools. One highly regarded, independent school on an adjoining property was faced with closure due to enrollment declines.

The West Town motto, "Find the spirit within yourself," captured the exceptional dynamism of the school and the pervasive view that "West Town is a real place, a real preparation for the real world." West Town's sustained development over the long term was matched by its capacity to undertake significant reform in the short term. In less than a year, and in the context of a labor dispute within the broader educational system when school innovation was essentially taboo, West Town undertook an initiative to improve mathematical achievement. It was immensely successful (see Table A.1 in Appendix A for details). This innovative reform was the focus of our research.

In tracing the success of the innovation, we identified three key forces. One was the initiative of Tom, the head of the mathematics department, and was based on his expressed love of mathematics as a discipline, on his capacity to negotiate behind the scenes on behalf of his department, and on his skill in mobilizing staff within his department in spite of the constraints brought about by the labor dispute.

A second force was the clear vision for the school held by Ray, the principal. He had a firm desire to ensure that West Town students have a sense of pride and identity usually reserved for independent-school students. And he supported his vision with dogged pursuit of complementary ideas and activities from the staff and community and a notable talent for down-to-earth talk with students, teachers, and parents. That he had been a former professional football player was helpful. His background, no doubt, contributed to the impression that he could "move mountains"—or, at least, walls and timetables—to facilitate the educational changes he supported.

The third force was the initiative of another mathematics teacher, Janiene, who organized after-school mathematics programs that brought highly competent resource persons, such as engineering students, into the school and engaged teachers in forms of tutorial, inquiry-oriented instruction that were new to many. However, her actions, motivated by a commitment to students and in response to the school's vision, brought her into a degree of conflict with some colleagues, despite her gentle demeanor and apolitical approach.

Evidence of significant progress and improved student outcomes as a result of the innovation is well documented. Its impact, however, stretched well beyond students' improved math scores. A new sense of confidence in mathematical thinking, heightened parental support for the school, and further enrollment increases—all were documented results of the innovation.

Yet just as the innovation's success was spreading, even in the face of labor union resistance to any effort beyond the ordinary, it came to an abrupt end. Ray, the principal, transferred to another school, leaving behind an altered political dynamic. New alliances were created that resulted in a withdrawal of administrative support for the innovation and a decision on the part of the department head to abandon it until such time as it could be appropriately funded and supported.

Several months later, when a permanent principal was appointed, the teacher leaders were successful in securing support for their project, and the initiative came to life again.

The principal's strategic role was of undoubted importance, as was the existence of professional trust on the part of the school's middle managers. The capacity of teacher leaders to negotiate change processes that involved serious political demands in addition to significant shifts in teaching and learning approaches was equally important. Most important, principal and teachers exercised leadership simultaneously.

Defining Parallel Leadership

The focus of this chapter is parallel leadership. It is a concept that derives from the breakthroughs of the past decade in the area of educational leadership as a shared professional responsibility, but it differs in two important regards. First, it affirms the sophistication of the teaching profession and thus sees the leadership of principals and teachers in school reform as similar in significance. Second, it recognizes the reality of today's schools as learning organizations. Accordingly, it assumes an inextricable link between school-based leadership and the enhancement of educational outcomes, a link that can be understood and articulated.

Definition of Parallel Leadership

Parallel leadership, as we define it, encourages a relatedness between teacher leaders and administrator leaders that activates and sustains the knowledge-generating capacity of schools: Parallel leadership is a process whereby teacher leaders and their principals engage in collective action to build school capacity. It embodies mutual respect, shared purpose, and allowance for individual expression.

Thus the power of parallel leadership resides in its connection to what King and Newmann (2000) call organizational capacity. As such, it has potential relevance for a wide range of postindustrial organizations, but it is most appropriate to schools, where the creation of meaning from teaching and learning constitutes the core business.

Our most recent research focused, in part, on ways that parallel leadership might spur changes leading to enhanced student outcomes: Tentative conclusions point to the importance of three intersecting processes—namely professional learning, culture building, and school-wide approaches to pedagogy. This chapter focuses on the critical role of parallel leadership in these foundational processes.

Three Essential Characteristics of Parallel Leadership

Parallel leadership, as we observed it, has three distinct characteristics: *mutualism, a sense of shared purpose,* and *allowance for individual expression*. The West Town High sketch makes clear the importance and specific meaning of these three defining characteristics.

Mutualism

Mutualism, in the form of mutual trust and respect between administrator leaders and teacher leaders, is a distinct feature of the workplace. It showed most clearly at West Town in each party's appreciation of the other's responsibilities. The result was the creation of an environment conducive to the generation of new ideas, reflective of a willingness to acknowledge and support others' ideas, and supportive of the application of others' proficiency.

Specifically, the strategic role of the principal and the expertise of teacher leaders at West Town were regarded as equally important and as interdependent in shaping and implementing innovation. The mathematics department head straddled both sets of functions and played a critical role in generating and sustaining trust. When, because of the change in principals, this trust was temporarily lost, the initiative ceased to function. Mutualism, as we have observed it, resembles what Bryk and Schneider (as cited in Fleming & Leo, 2000) refer to as relational trust:

> Relational trust creates an environment where individuals share a moral commitment to act in the interests of the collectivity, and this ethical basis for individual action constitutes a moral resource that the institution can draw on to initiate and sustain change. (p. 4)

For teachers, the issue of relatedness has long-standing significance. Building on the work of Lortie (1975), numerous researchers have illuminated ways that teachers have found the isolation of their work not only alienating but also very difficult to redress. Lieberman, Saxl, and Miles (1988), for example, showed how genuine professional collegiality in a school is founded on trust and rapport, whereas Hargreaves (1994) asserted that the establishment of trust is central to the restructuring of school systems that strive to enter a postmodern paradigm: "The challenge [is] building confidence and connectedness among teachers who may not know each other quite so well, by investing mutual trust in complementary expertise—without this also leading to burgeoning bureaucracy" (p. 254).

Fleming and Leo (2000) believe, on the basis of research into trust building and teacher efficacy, that professional learning communities can be stimulated. From these researchers and others, we know that both staff and students benefit from the presence of professional learning communities in schools. Teachers are less isolated, share in the collective responsibility for student success, and have higher morale and lower absenteeism. Students in these schools also have greater academic gains, and there are smaller achievement gaps between students of different backgrounds (King & Newmann, 2000; Newmann & Wehlage, 1995).

A Sense of Shared Purpose

Also noticeable in the West Town snapshot—and in all of our case studies where teacher leadership and parallel leadership were flourishing—is a sense of shared purpose. The observed effect was an alignment between the school's stated vision and the teachers' preferred approaches to teaching, learning, and assessment. Teacher leaders invariably assumed major responsibility for this alignment, both in their teaching of students and in their own learning as professionals. Administrator leaders (usually, but not always, including the principal) tended to assume major responsibility for strategic functions, including visioning, integrative planning, distribution of power, transformation of culture, and the development of external alliances.

The evolution of a distinctive school culture—reflecting the integration of the school vision and schoolwide approaches to teaching, learning, and assessment—has been noted by a number of authoritative critics, including Sergiovanni (1998) and Senge (as cited in O'Neill, 1995) as the foundation for sustained school improvement and success. In our case studies, this phenomenon appeared to have its origins in a shared commitment to values, such as the integrity of teaching or the need for social justice. At West Town, for example, the principal, Ray, and teacher leader, Janiene, articulated personal convictions regarding the need for disadvantaged students to experience a strong sense of pride in their communities and backgrounds. The net effect of the shared purpose that we observed in all of the case studies was an alignment between the school's stated vision and teachers' preferred approaches to teaching. This alignment appeared to ease the way for structural and curriculum change.

A sense of shared purpose did not, however, mean compromising values. To the contrary, the negotiation between teacher leaders and principal was prompted by a common perception that West Town's vision and its teaching approaches were out of alignment. The intense dialogue sharpened awareness—and appreciation—of value differences among staff and even led to the development of a common language in the school about teaching and learning. This helped the staff lay the foundation for a school culture that was more transparent and that more clearly encompassed the diversity of values in the school.

Allowance for Individual Expression

The third characteristic that we discerned in our case studies may appear, at first glance, to fly in the face of much recent thinking about school reform: allowance for individual expression. Observed relationships between teacher leaders and principals allowed for, even encouraged, a high degree of individual expression and action. This phenomenon may be inconsistent with recent emphases on teamwork, collegiality, and collaboration in educational workplaces. But the leaders and their allies had strong convictions about individual values as well as a capacity to accommodate the values of others. Thus shared leadership was associated with recognition of strong, skilled, autonomous individuals and with collaboration among them rather than with consensus within groups. Hargreaves's (1994) distinction between individualism, which connotes isolation and solitude, and individuality, which connotes personal independence and self-realization, is one that we have found very helpful. What we observed as individual expression and action is more akin to individuality than to individualism. At West Town, for example, Janiene and Tom were publicly acknowledged as the initiators of the innovative mathematics initiative undertaken despite labor dissent. Staff members praised the principal's support of public education while, at the same time, severely criticizing him for his support of a highly contentious state policy imperative.

Participants in the cases we studied asserted individual values and took individual responsibility more than is likely when collegial consensus is emphasized. Implicit, at times, in this individual assertiveness and activism was a suspicion of teamwork as open to managerial manipulation and control—a suspicion that has been well captured by a number of authors including Wilkins and Ouchi in 1983 (as cited in Sinclair, 1995, p. 48), and Hargreaves (1994).

On the basis of our research to date, we are inclined to agree with Limerick, Cunnington, and Crowther (1998) that collective processes that serve to obscure individuality are more likely to contribute to the perpetuation of questionable practices on the part of both principals and teachers than are processes that recognize individual action and the legitimacy of dissent. Thus parallel leadership poses immense challenges for leadership and organizational development.

The demands on principals to accept and accommodate potential teacher leaders ("stirrers," to use a colloquial expression from one of our sites) are obvious if the legitimacy of strong individual action is accepted—as it is by a number of authorities, including Boomer (1985), who has applauded "teaching against the grain" (p. 20); Shor and Freire (1987), who espouse teaching for liberation; and Gutierrez, Rymes, and Larson (1995), who speak of teachers searching for the "third space." The effects of individuality may, therefore, be too much for some principals to accommodate, but principals in our case studies recognized its value and built on it.

In summary, parallel leadership engages teacher leaders and administrator leaders in collaborative action while, at the same time, encouraging fulfillment of their individual capabilities, aspirations, and responsibilities. It leads to strengthened alignment between the school's vision and the school's teaching, learning, and assessment practices. It facilitates professional learning, culture building, and schoolwide approaches to pedagogy. It makes possible the enhancement of school identity, teachers' professional esteem, community support, and students' achievements.

Parallelism in the Sciences, Arts, and Humanities

In advancing parallelism as a professionally appropriate approach to school-based leadership, we acknowledge, first of all, its dictionary definition: "agreement in direction, tendency or character" (Macquarie Library, 1998, p. 1560). Essential to our developmental work, however, have been the rich and complex meanings of this concept in a number of fields of cultural and intellectual endeavor.

Consider, for example, the field of *music*, where parallelism connotes the harmony derived when two independent parts or voices within a musical texture move up or down by the same distance in tandem (e.g., parallel fifths). In *language,* parallelism is well known. For example, analogies allow new meaning to be constructed through correspondence between two different concepts. In the world of *mathematics,* parallelism refers to forces that mirror each other. Parallel lines, for example, sustain their individual identities while maintaining a common direction and an unwavering distance from each other. In *computer science*, parallel processing refers to the management of complex data through systems that operate in a complementary fashion. Finally, consider the discipline of *philosophy*, in particular metaphysics, where parallelism connotes a doctrine of mind and body interacting synchronistically while remaining independent.

Parallelism in these human endeavors suggests qualities such as harmony, direction, alignment, and mutuality. These qualities bear striking resemblance to the distinctive form of educational leadership that we have observed between teacher leaders and administrator leaders in our case studies.

How Parallel Leadership Works

In the final phase of our research, we focused primarily on the dynamics that occur as schools engage successfully in revitalization and reform. As mentioned above, we and our colleagues traced the experiences of nine schools that initiated and managed processes resulting in documented evidence of enhanced student achievement in literacy or mathematics (Crowther, Hann, & McMaster, 2001). When a school's professional community engages in schoolwide pedagogical development and, at the same time, works toward development of a distinctive identity, it maximizes its capacity to enhance outcomes, particularly student achievement. Figure 3.1 shows how parallel leadership engages processes of professional learning, culture building, and schoolwide pedagogy to enhance a school's overall capacity to produce positive student outcomes. While this link between parallel leadership and improved outcomes is tenuous, substantiated only by case study research at this juncture, it represents a potentially significant connection deserving further research and analysis.

Figure 3.1. Linking Parallel Leadership and Successful School Reform

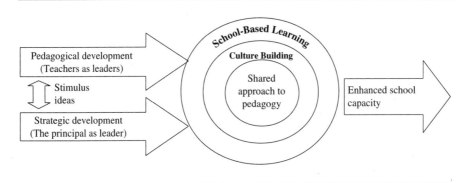

Professional Learning

As we observed it in schools that managed processes of revitalization with substantial success, professional learning invariably involved principals and teachers in joint professional development activities. The customary separation of principal development and teacher development was largely rejected in these schools and replaced by ongoing joint inquiry that enhances the alignment of the school's vision with schoolwide approaches to teaching, learning, and assessment.

Sunbeach School is one example where the principal (Paul) and a teacher leader (Loretta) worked in parallel to develop professional learning opportunities that fostered such schoolwide approaches. Opportunities like these invariably prompt principals and teachers to create together new operating assumptions. Students are the inevitable beneficiaries of such efforts wherever they occur (Argyris & Schon, 1996).

At Sunbeach, collaboration and a shared sense of purpose were integral to the actions of both the teacher leader and the principal. Whereas Loretta articulated her vision about the literacy program, Paul articulated ways to approach the staff and to align the program with the school's vision. At staff meetings, teachers became acquainted with the program, defended their own programs based on their own teaching values and philosophies, aired concerns, and suggested ways to incorporate the proposal into their teaching. Furthermore, Loretta and other teachers seized an opportunity to take part in a national project, guided by university researchers, that engaged them in action research and opened them to significant professional learning.

Bringing together teachers, administrators, and policy makers in this way had one other powerful effect. It helped sustain the reform despite changeovers in staff, including the principal. When professional learning is communal, the school's core values gain heightened importance, and role-based authority assumes a supportive and facilitative role rather than a directive one.

Culture Building

The second process that is essential to successful school revitalization and that can be activated and nurtured through parallel leadership is culture building. Most of our insights about this concept are drawn from our studies in Catholic schools, although we have concluded that the culture-building capacity of public schools is just as great as that of private and religious schools. Of relevance here is Sergiovanni's (1998) claim: "Schools with character have unique cultures. They know who they are and have developed a common understanding of their purposes. They celebrate their uniqueness as a powerful way to achieve their goals" (p. 88). Also significant is Senge's (1992; 2000) claim that if organizational learning is to become organizational knowledge then "the group" must find its own ways of bridging the gap: for example, by developing understanding of the perspectives of different groups in the school, building new lines of communication, respecting people's inhibitions about personal change, and allowing a flexible and tolerant culture to evolve. Through parallel leadership, the cultural values and beliefs that underpin the school vision and that may be assumed to reflect the needs and priorities of the broader community, can be integrated purposefully and naturally with the dynamics of teachers' work—why they teach the way they do, what they aspire to individually and collectively, and the concepts and processes of their programs. At Greenhills High (snapshot in Chapter 1), for example, a tangible school culture grew from a shared goal to build advantage from disadvantage. A perceived need to create a strong sense of identity challenged the teachers to align their teaching practices and programs to that of identity building. From this grew a strong sense of pride among students, who began to "hold their heads up."

The three elements of Schein's (1992) cultural model (*artifacts, values, assumptions*) can be identified at Greenhills. *Artifacts* (students' pride in wearing the school uniform, celebrations at school assemblies) were readily observable. Espoused *values*, such as high expectations and positive community relationships, were evident in the school's policy, strategic plan, and behavior-management plan. The *assumption* that socioeconomic disadvantage need be no barrier to success was reflected in statements like, "We can do anything," and "Every student has a gift." Moreover, in referring to the school's achievements and teachers' roles, the principal used terms like " the guardians of our culture." In so doing, he illustrated the integration of artifacts, values, and assumptions within the school and their links to both the school vision and teachers' expertise.

Our case studies contain the strong implication that all members of the school community should view themselves as able to contribute to culture building, but that teachers are central to this endeavor.

This brief description of school culture building would not be complete without a mention of language. In our case studies of successful school reform, teachers tended to reject the language of hierarchy (e.g., "I'm just a teacher," "my superior," "my subordinates," "let's see what the boss wants," "just tell me what to do and I'll do it," " I came here for the express purpose of turning this school around," "my school staff"). Principals accepted teacher leadership even where the language to support this new concept was not readily available. In other words, teachers and principals alike demonstrated a capacity for participatory democracy that suggests schools might lead the way into the postindustrial era (Glickman, 1998; Goodlad as cited in Goldberg, 2000).

Schoolwide Approaches to Pedagogy

The third of the three intersecting processes—schoolwide approaches to pedagogy—is important not only in our studies but also in other recent research, including the University of Wisconsin's Center on Organization and Restructuring of Schools (CORS) project, whose purpose is to explore ways to use restructuring to elevate student learning. Where school reform involves collective responsibility for an agreed-on approach to teaching, learning, and assessment, it directly and significantly affects student achievement, especially for students from lower socioeconomic backgrounds. In this regard, we endorse Senge's (as cited in O'Neill, 1995) powerful assertion that "You cannot implement 'learner-directed learning,' for example, in one classroom and not others. It would drive the kids nuts, not to mention the stress on the individual teacher" (p. 21).

But how can the numerous individual pedagogical preferences of teachers be brought together into a schoolwide approach? In our view, only through processes that fly squarely in the face of most school organizational practices of the past 100 years. Schoolwide approaches to teaching, learning, and assessment develop only when parallel leadership is in place—when teacher leaders assume responsibility for identifying critical commonalities in their most successful individual teaching practices and then, in conjunction with their principals, either align those common practices with the school's vision or negotiate meaningful changes in the vision.

Bordertown teachers' individual priorities at the outset of their reform process included the following:

- Academic skill development

- Interpersonal problem solving

- Community building

- Lifelong learning

- Environmental sustainability

- Holistic development of the individual

- Preparation for a technological world

- Vocational preparation

- Moral development

Successful classroom practices in each of these areas were explored in relation to the school vision and were distilled over a period of months into the schoolwide principles contained in Table 2.1. Thus the ground was laid for the transformation of the school's public image, enhancement of teachers' sense of professionalism, and, according to preliminary evidence, improvement in student outcomes.

Through the integration of processes of professional learning, culture building, and schoolwide approaches to educational reform, the school's distinctive identity is enhanced, thereby sharpening the focus of professional practice and creating a foundation for educational renewal.

Conclusions

In this chapter, we drew on the most recent developments in educational leadership as well as on our research-based observations of teacher leaders and their principals at work to develop a new educational concept, that of parallel leadership. We substantiate our claims about the integrity of this new concept by exploring its meanings in a number of fields of cultural and intellectual endeavor and by teasing out its underpinning values. Extending these analyses, we link parallel leadership with processes that contribute to successful school reform and thus enhance school capacity to produce positive outcomes. Our Diagram Linking Parallel Leadership and Successful School Reform (Figure 3.1) is a visual image of this linkage that we believe contributes to overcoming a major impediment to current approaches to successful school-based innovation.

CHAPTER 4

New Roles for School Principals

The Principal's Role: Change Is Overdue

Traditionally, as has been discussed, school-based leadership has centered on the role of the principal. As shown in our review in Chapter 2 of the four different forms of educational leadership, it is difficult to separate the evolution of leadership concepts in education from principals' work. Tyack and Honsot wrote in 1982 (as cited in Smith & Ellett, 2000, p. 1) that some observers also claim that, in addition to being regarded almost universally as the superordinate position in the school, the role of the principal has changed little during the past century. This stasis has been maintained, according to Cuban (as cited in Smith and Ellet, 2000, p. 1) in 1984, even though there have been waves of reform aimed at reshaping principals' and teachers' roles.

As might be expected, most available leadership development resources deal with preparing school principals. Not surprisingly, therefore, educational leadership programs in recent decades have tended to view the principal's role in terms of strategic processes like goal setting, needs identification, priority setting, policy making, planning, budgeting, and evaluation (Caldwell, 1992, p. 16) or of operational functions like program implementation, staff supervision, and conflict management (Heifetz & Laurie, 1997).

To some observers (Bates, 1992; Gronn, 1999), this emphasis on the principalship as the center of educational leadership is ill directed and occurs at the expense of the image and esteem of teachers. Even those who argue that the principal's role has undergone massive change during the past 30 years—for example, from manager to instructional leader to transformational or transactional leader—generally agree that the role has retained a common thread through the decades. Moreover, leadership theory is characterized by a centrist perspective, in which the principal is viewed as the center of school decision making, authority, and action. Each theory could be said to reify the great-leader paradigm evident in the early literature on leadership.

The Role of the Principal in Successful School Reform

Phase three of our research involved a series of workshops with principals and teacher leaders. The workshops' purpose was to examine the leadership of schools that had engaged in successful reform. We quickly came to question long-held views of a centrist role for principals. Our case studies disclosed that principals in these schools employed management and leadership strategies that were not easily explained through the traditional paradigm. Although we could see in their work attention to such processes as policy development, priority setting, budgeting, and conflict management, we discerned much more.

Observable processes, basic to the exercise of parallel leadership, reflected mutualism, shared direction, and individual expression. Additional processes bore clear resemblance to postindustrial leadership approaches, such as those that Mintzberg (1994) referred to as *strategic thinking* and that Limerick, Cunnington, and Crowther (1998) called *metastrategy*. In essence, the role of the principal, as we observed it in our case studies of successful school reform, encompassed five functions:

Visioning links developmental work in schools with an inspiring image of a preferred future, making obvious the connection between innovation and collective creation of the school's future.

Identity generation promotes creation of cultural meaning. Two important goals are served. First, communities can view their schools as distinctive (or differentiated) and can regard themselves as instruments for creating a distinctive culture and system of meaning. Second, a benchmark is set whereby members of both the school and the broader community determine whether the envisaged future is consistent with their values. If not, they can consider ways to change it.

Alignment of organizational elements fosters the holistic implementation of school-based innovations. Where the rationale for an innovation is aligned with the school's vision, where there are schoolwide approaches to pedagogy, where school infrastructures (time, space, curricula, and technologies) have been modified to facilitate implementation, and where the professional community has a shared understanding of—and commitment to—the essential features of an innovation, the basis for successful implementation is strong.

Distribution of power and leadership encourages teachers (and community members) to view themselves as important in shaping the school's direction and values and in exercising influence beyond the school.

External alliances and networking allow schools to collaborate with other schools and with the broader community while keeping for themselves activities that reflect their distinctive competencies. Examples are *consortia,* in which schools pool their resources to gain a benefit that they could not acquire alone; *joint ventures,* in which several schools pursue an opportunity that requires a special capacity from each; and *value chain partnerships,* in which organizations in different industries—say, education and tourism—with different but complementary skills link their capabilities to create value for ultimate users.

Taken together, these five functions provide a sound basis for principals aspiring to lead their schools in the years ahead. But none of the functions is realizable without parallel leadership. Hence none is possible without teacher leadership. Thus the fundamental question of this chapter becomes, "What is the principal's role in nurturing teacher leadership?"

Nurturing Teacher Leadership: Seven Challenges for School Principals

Our interviews with case study principals revealed a wide range of strategies that they employed to nurture teacher leaders in their schools and to develop mature parallel-leader relationships. From this range of strategies, we identified seven broad challenges that confronted them and that they appeared to meet successfully. As they did so, the intersecting processes of schoolwide pedagogy, culture building, and professional learning were activated and sustained, and school capacity was enhanced.

Each challenge is described below, with illustrative quotations taken from the case studies. As becomes evident, the seven challenges are, in some ways, at considerable odds with time-honored views of the principalship. That said, our research suggests that the nurturing of teacher leadership is a function that most school principals will embrace enthusiastically because of its potential to contribute to the maturation of the teaching profession and as a result of its links to school capacity building.

Challenge One: Communicate Strategic Intent

> A comment from a case study principal: "You have to build up in kids the notion that what they do is important. My guiding philosophy here is, 'Students for the future and a future for our students.'"

> A teacher leader's response: "I'd say, without a shadow of doubt, that he has a passionate attachment to what we are doing. He believes that we can make a difference. There's no passing the buck here, starting with the principal. Personal responsibility is always on show."

To nurture teacher leadership, principals need to be unambiguous about their strategic intent. If the principal's educational worldview is apparent through words and deeds, potential teacher leaders have a model for futuristic thinking about their workplace and can reflect, explore, and experiment through their teaching.

The principals we studied cultivated a clear sense of purpose in their schools and generated broad systems of action to support that purpose. They made their essential educational convictions explicit through their public and professional presentations. For example, the principal of Greenhills High reiterated the school motto—"Success breeds success"—on a regular basis in his descriptions of school projects. And he encouraged teachers and students to develop their own, personalized versions of that motto (the "We can do anything" motto of the student body originated in this way). The principal of West Town High, a school on the other side of the tracks, used the phrase "the hero within" to demonstrate his conviction that students from the school had unique talents that would enable them to achieve their aspirations in an exciting future world.

The explication of a clear statement of purpose enables teachers, parents, and students to understand and explain the values that guide the work of their principals. In our case studies, teachers understood and accepted that significant responsibilities went with the position of principal, including duty of care (stewardship of the students), trustee of public property and resources, and guardian of due process (or natural justice). They also knew that educational commitment, in and of itself, was valued. Thus the basis for deep professional respect was laid.

Principals who declare themselves in this way can, of course, be vulnerable if they do not manage dissonance skillfully, because the strength of their personal values is unlikely to suit all persons and all situations. But by making their views and patterns of action transparent, they demonstrate that visioning is an exciting and important school-based strategy for all leaders, both practicing and aspiring, whether they occupy formal or informal leader roles.

Challenge Two: Incorporate the Aspirations and Views of Others

> A comment from a case study principal: "I have to ensure that when someone who is entrepreneurial comes up with a good idea, that idea *can* fit under the umbrella of the school vision. If it *can*, let's just see where it can go. Passion has to drive ideas or they lose momentum, so projects should be run by those who are most passionate."

> A teacher leader's response: "She listens. She tries consciously to locate us in the context of where the school is going. I think it gives her a real buzz to see teachers developing new skills and getting recognition as leaders."

The concept of *collective intelligence* has been proposed by theorists Heifetz and Laurie (1997) as integral to organizational problem solving. That is to say, when senior executives draw on the ideas and energy of colleagues from throughout their organizations, they not only engender more creative solutions but also build trust and commitment that they can call on in the future. In this way, the capacity-building potential of the organization is enhanced.

Principals in successful parallel leadership relationships act on this principle. They spend time and energy soliciting ideas and encouraging teachers and community members to view themselves as critically important in shaping the school's direction and values. As principals do this, potential teacher leaders gain important opportunities to clarify and refine their personal values. They also gain a sense of confidence to develop projects that they believe in but might otherwise not develop. Thus the leadership potential of others, most notably teachers, is acknowledged, encouraged, and nurtured.

In one of our case study schools, the principal inherited a situation that was characterized by both conflict and atrophy. Her statement of strategic intent ("to create a spiritual environment where everyone achieves success") struck a resonant chord in the school community and triggered a series of constructive, within-school programs and community volunteer initiatives. Within the short space of 2 years, her original vision had been modified significantly ("to be a place where everyone has choices and everyone is responsible for what we achieve"), and teacher leaders carried much of the responsibility for the ongoing development of the school. In the words of one young teacher, "Anyone here can lead. It's just a matter of having ideas that fit our school goals and following through."

In another case study, the principal made overt, significant adjustments to the school's vision when it became apparent that the one he had crafted did not do full justice to schoolwide teaching approaches that the staff had developed. One teacher, who was instrumental in establishing a nationally recognized literacy program at the school, asserted that "Peter [the principal] is a great communicator. The way he listens, we know that our ideas can go somewhere. It makes us eager to sort out our priorities and get on and do new things."

The enrichment of personal vision is, therefore, a complex and challenging process. It requires deliberate dialogue, reference to diverse value systems, careful listening, and, of course, an enthusiasm for enriching one's own professional values. It also requires skill in synthesizing messages that, in some cases, may be subtle or even unspoken. These proficiencies were not necessarily required in previous, less complex education systems, but they are essential in education systems where the generation of new knowledge is a key function.

Of significance is the conclusion discussed in Chapter 3 that it is largely through the integration of the principal's strategic intent with teachers' views and aspirations that the school's vision and teaching practices are brought into alignment. Authoritative research (King & Newmann, 2000) reveals that this integration provides a strong foundation for enhanced school capacity. Principals in our case studies understood this and approached the processes of whole-school reform and whole-school leader development as one and the same.

Challenge Three: Pose Difficult-to-Answer Questions

A comment from a case study principal: "I might go around to the classrooms and ask the teachers questions like, 'What if? I wonder what . . .?' It's not what I want but what can be done that matters. In the staff room one day, I posed the question, 'What might a meaningful metaphor look like for this school?' Someone suggested that we all write our responses on the discussion board over a period of time, and out of that, we developed a metaphor together."

A teacher leader's response: "What he does is listen to the silences in people and draw out their ideas. If you are going to think outside the box, you have to believe that your ideas are going to be valued. That really happens here. No topic is taboo if kids' well-being is the motivation."

Individual expression is fundamental to parallel leadership. It is a value that is grounded in respect for individuality and that implies a regard for questioning rather than inculcation and for consciousness raising rather than the imposition of dictates. Its significance for school leaders in a knowledge society is clear in Drucker's (as cited in Andersen Consulting Institute for Strategic Change, 1999) provocative, though simple, assertion that "leaders of the future will be people who know how to ask rather than tell" (p. 2).

We observed this orientation to open-ended inquiry in our case studies when, for example, one principal invited staff members to create metaphors for the school's leadership, both as they experienced it and as they would like to experience it. A small group of teachers used the results to generate a whole-school leadership framework. In another case, the principal used the question, "How can we make our teaching approach obvious to anyone who looks?" in order to stimulate a serious critique of both teaching practices and of the school's vision that "we are a school for the 21st century." Such questions do not require answers in advance but rather the capacity to explore the world that lies outside our immediate consciousness.

Posing difficult-to-answer questions makes clear to the professional community of the school, and also to the wider community, that taking an informed stance on an issue is valued. This will invariably include dialogue about a range of complex and unforeseeable matters relating to equity, justice, ecology, tolerance, and so on. It also means that the taken-for-granted practices of the workplace—including language, artifacts, slogans, and behaviors—are continuously open to challenge. Because many of these practices may have originated with a principal or teachers of long standing in the community, honoring tough questions, when posed, requires not only maturity and confidence but also courage and patience. In one case study school, the questioning of the school's slogan—"Pride of the Peninsula"—led to consideration of the hidden messages for other schools in the area. Eventually, the slogan was ratified, but only after a school-based theory of learning, grounded in values of tolerance and global citizenship, was developed to justify it.

Although posing and investigating tough questions enables teachers to explore their pedagogical beliefs and values, and stimulates opportunities for meaningful professional learning, it, nevertheless, can create complex dilemmas for principals. They must engage the full professional community of the school, starting with themselves, in a continuous questioning of the school's practices. And they must attempt to develop awareness of the big picture that, according to Senge (2000), is exceedingly rare in schools. Its absence constitutes a major impediment in the creation of learning organizations.

One might suppose that continuous critical analysis of this type would lead to unrestrained autonomous behavior, even anarchy. To the contrary, teachers in our case study schools responded enthusiastically to opportunities to uncover hidden values in their schools and to clarify their tacit beliefs regarding their work as teachers. One effect was the emergence of distinctive forms of teacher leadership, frequently involving professionals who had not previously seen themselves as leaders and who, in some cases, had been regarded as troublemakers or burrs under the saddle. In sum, principals who encourage questioning in this way lay the foundations for the emergence of a cadre of leaders who might otherwise remain obscure and for the creation of forms of knowledge that would not otherwise be possible.

Challenge Four: Make Space for Individual Innovation

A comment from a case study principal: "I tell people that I promote risk and, if something gets up to 90 percent and falls over, then I take the rap for that. If it goes well though, the teacher gets all the credit. Playing it safe and by the book might protect you as a principal, but it can lead to stultification of the school. In this current world, you either move forward or you decline in quality."

A teacher leader's response: "We often spend time at meetings just thinking up crazy ideas. Then we talk about 'How?' So you are constantly reminded of just how serious teaching is as a profession. You know that where there's a good idea to take the school forward, a way will be found to do it."

Potential teacher leaders (and a high proportion of practicing teacher leaders) are seldom, in our experience, aware of their leadership capabilities. Nor are they aware of the strength or nature of their individual styles, in terms of personality, teaching approach, or leadership. Thus opportunities and encouragement to explore and express their talents in a relatively safe environment, both as individuals and in groups, are essential for their development and maturation. This is particularly so because the exercise of teacher leadership invariably involves confronting cultural, social, physical, professional, and psychological barriers. The political and personal skills that are required to overcome institutional obstacles appear to us to be most easily learned in environments where trust, security, and confidence are present.

Principals in our case studies recognized this need and indicated a sense of professional responsibility to respond to it. In one school where parallel leadership flourished, an administrator-adopted school code reminded teachers that assistance was available to address the following questions:

How can we help remove obstacles in your way?

How can we build on the positives in your innovation?

How can we create strong links between your work and the school's vision?

Our case studies revealed at least three broad ways in which principals encouraged innovative action and thus nurtured leadership within the professional community of the school. In several instances, principals identified individual teachers, or small groups of teachers, for leadership of priority school projects and then made themselves available as mentors. In other instances, they encouraged staff members to nominate colleagues to develop innovative ideas and, subsequently, accorded the nominees wide responsibility in following through on those ideas. In other situations, individual teachers proposed initiatives, usually focusing on innovative teaching and learning, and found their administrators not only supportive but forthcoming with advice as to how to overcome infrastructural barriers and to link the initiatives in question to the school vision.

Obvious in these examples is that principals in the case studies frequently encouraged teacher individualism to an extent that seems to counter recent trends in organizational development favoring collegiality and team processes. For example, in one school, teachers were encouraged to use professional development opportunities to transpose the agreed-on schoolwide teaching approaches into classroom practices that emphasized individual teachers' personal teaching styles and enabled them to share their personal strengths with others.

What emerged was a range of strategies that, at one and the same time, reinforced the agreed-on pedagogical principles of the school and demonstrated the versatility of those principles. Compelling relationships among personal teaching styles, schoolwide approaches to pedagogy, and leadership concepts became apparent as a result of this exercise. Based on experiences of this type, we agree with Kofman and Senge (1993) that it is through recognition of individual talents and learning that processes of "personal transformation" and of overcoming fear of the unknown are set in motion (pp. 5, 19).

The question of how to encourage innovation and discourage unfocused effort, a mishmash of unrelated activities, and energy-sapping competition for scarce resources is also important for principals looking for ways to make space for teacher leaders. It is our experience that where the school community agrees on the vision for the school, and where the purpose of innovation is to enhance the alignment of teaching practices with that vision, such wastage can be minimized if not totally avoided.

Where potentially powerful ideas are identified early and supported through resource and infrastructure alignment, the likelihood that potential teacher leaders will look to innovation with confidence and enthusiasm increases. Thus principals who make a point of making space for innovation serve several purposes at once. They enhance the alignment of key school processes—most notably, vision, teaching practices, and infrastructure; they broaden and deepen the leadership capacity of the school; and they enhance the stature of the teaching profession. The net effect is the creation of change from within, a hallmark of sustained school success.

Challenge Five: Know When to Step Back

A comment from a case study principal: "I have had to learn how to advance my own interests by stepping back. It's a subtle act of leadership and one you can learn easily by capitalizing on people's strengths. It helps you sustain what you have helped to create."

A teacher leader's response: "She has a habit of asking, 'Have you asked Joe or Mary what they think?' It's amazing how this brings quiet leaders out of the woodwork. She never assumes that she's the best at anything."

Teacher leadership is inseparable from the concept of empowerment, which is usually characterized as involvement in organizational decision making (Rice & Schneider, 1994). Because empowerment has been seen for several decades as critical to the creation of a learning organization (Argyris & Schon, 1979), it follows that principals who want to see their schools develop as learning organizations must empower their teachers in meaningful ways. In effect, they must know how and when to step back from their own leader roles and, in so doing, to encourage teacher colleagues to step forward. This may present immense challenges in terms of ego disengagement and the learning of new skills regarding power sharing. But if potential teacher leaders are to be encouraged in their work, and if opportunities are to be created for them to further develop their leadership capabilities, then stepping back is a critically important strategy for a principal to adopt.

At some of the schools where we observed parallel leadership in place, shifts in curriculum and teaching practices were orchestrated by a school management team chaired by a teacher who received assistance from an external facilitator. Significantly, these teams did not answer to the principal; rather, the principal was usually a team member. This strategy served to provide important structural support for teachers undertaking significant leadership roles. It also demonstrated that power sharing among co-professionals is important. Critically, it made explicit that teaching and learning were central to the school operations and should be managed by teachers. Potential teacher leaders invariably rose to the occasion when presented with this level of confidence and trust.

In developing the capacity to step back, principals should keep in mind that leadership may be a less visible phenomenon when it is vested in several people instead of one. Individual leadership is undoubtedly easier to spot than distributed leadership. Our culture is laden with clichés about single leaders, such as "it's lonely at the top," "leading from the front," "down in the trenches," "a born leader," or "the buck stops here." All reflect an outmoded, industrial-age paradigm. New images of postindustrial forms of leadership are not yet incorporated into our thought processes or our vocabulary, although we have made a start. For example, one authoritative commentator observed that words and phrases such as *healing, please, common ground,* and *restora-*

tion constitute a "language of potential" for leaders in service-oriented organizations (De Pree, 1997, p. 74). We suggest that "step to the back as the occasion requires" expresses the sort of leadership that should become part of everyday school practice, and, therefore, should also become part of our vocabulary.

Metaphors from both educational and noneducational settings can communicate that stepping back does not constitute an abrogation of leadership. It constitutes a mature professional stance. One case study school adopted the familiar metaphor of geese flying in V-formation (taking turns with the energy-sapping lead spot; maintaining alignment to maximize airlift; taking time out to look after injured, weak, or fallen co-travelers; honking from the rear to provide encouragement to those carrying the major burden) to express the form of shared leadership that they adopted. Another chose the concept of "swooping onto loose balls," a term used in some team sports, to illustrate that at their school, any major problem that arose had to be addressed collectively.

Stepping back, with the sense of teacher empowerment that it implies, is fundamental to the development of shared leadership. But it is also at odds with the dominant conceptions of the principalship that have been in place in most education systems for decades. It, therefore, poses a significant challenge for principals.

Challenge Six: Create Opportunities From Perceived Difficulties

A comment from a case study principal: "In a complex place like a school, we can't always do everything right. But we can usually do the right thing. If we do the right thing and make a mistake, we can ask what went wrong and learn from the experience. I'm not saying we should go out of our way to make honest mistakes, but I am saying that honest mistakes can usually be used as valuable learning experiences."

A teacher leader's response: "The community was very politically divided at the time. His management of the different groups ensured that the feelings of animosity didn't spill over onto the playground. It was a learning experience for the whole community."

The following scenario from a case study school is an example of how one principal was able to transpose a difficult problem into an opportunity and, ultimately, into success. The principal at Palms School was faced with a difficult problem—how to persuade a number of alienated, homeless young people to attend school.

Some students, several from indigenous backgrounds, were causing serious disruption in the community, especially around shopping centers. The principal had been subjected to considerable personal and professional attack and was faced with the choice of whether to leave the community, transfer blame for the problem somewhere else, or tackle it head on. Without the overt support of educational or social agencies, most of which had been quite hostile, he allocated funds and engaged a teacher who was considered, in some circles, an instigator because of her political involvements. She was known to have deep empathy for the youth group—as well as exceptional teaching talent.

Within a year, she successfully brought the group into her confidence and set up a shopping-center point of contact. She worked on developing values associated with both indigenous and nonindigenous cultures and on building relationships with local merchants. Financial support was forthcoming as delinquency rates dropped, and political support followed. The project achieved national recognition and set a precedent that a number of other school communities followed. The teacher subsequently became a significant figure in representing alienated youth.

In schools where risk taking is encouraged and where leadership involves continuous journeys into the unknown, errors invariably will be made, blame ascribed, and problems unknowingly created. Our experience with schools in which parallel leadership has been in evidence is that errors and problems per se do not necessarily amount to obstacles or serious liabilities in the school's quest for excellence. To the contrary, where leadership is distributed and held together by trust and shared purpose, errors and difficulties can often be transposed into educational opportunities.

For this to occur, however, the principal's role must contain a distinctive leadership dimension. An environment of no blame—in which processes, not people, are scrutinized when things go wrong—must be created. Outside influences and pressures that have the potential to become immutable constraints must be managed, and accountability must be viewed as "for us" rather than "for you."

One effect of an attitude that says, "We don't have problems, just opportunities," is that the efforts of instigators can more readily be turned to advantage. Another is that thinking outside the box is encouraged and problem solving assumes an intellectually provocative dimension. A third is that underlying institutional barriers are exposed, thereby heightening the level and authenticity of professional dialogue. As these strategies become part of the school's way of doing things, the potential for teacher leaders to express themselves and to assume responsibility is enhanced.

In another of the case study schools, a chronic school drop-out problem was used to obtain funding to create a community-building project. Not only was the issue of student retention addressed with some notable effects, but the project also became a landmark that symbolized a new "we can do it" attitude in both school and community. The principal's success at showing how the project affected community pride, raised consciousness about the dynamics of complex problem solving, and drew attention to a range of previously unnoticed leadership talents in the school and wider community. Ultimately, his initiative had the effect of changing the school's approach to teaching. The small group of teachers who took the project forward became recognized as central to the well-being of the community. The complexities of mediating the environment of the school, inside and out—of adopting a can-do attitude against the odds, of creating networks and alliances to maximize the benefit of the school's distinctive resources, of stretching accepted boundaries to meet needs—can convince even inveterate doubters that it is possible to prevail on behalf of the educational needs of children. Schools where complex difficulties are used as a spur to collaborative learning can come to be regarded as models of positive problem solving and sources of hope. Through this plausible alternative to the prevailing norm, teachers begin to assume the mantle of what Drucker (1994, p. 64) called a "leading class."

Challenge Seven: Build on Achievements
to Create a Culture of Success

A comment from a case study principal: "You can have the greatest curriculum in the state, but unless you have a culture of hope, aspirations, recognition of successes, and directing kids towards success, then the whole thing can fall over."

A teacher leader's response: "Kids enroll here because they believe this school will give them a stamp. We don't need expensive PR. The principal goes out of his way to describe for them what that stamp looks like and how dynamic it is."

Teachers feel that they are building something, and they look for ways to add to it. For a range of complex reasons, the real achievements of many schools are not used to major advantage as much and as often as they could be. Few schools consider how they have influenced students' lives, or community well-being, in definitive and positive ways, and then proceed to provide documented evidence of their achievements. Most schools do not regard it as a high priority to generate a public image of a culture of success. In failing to do so, they undersell their contributions to the broader community and discourage initiative on the part of committed, energetic teachers.

In pursuing this point in the schools we studied, we were told that some principals might be reluctant to emphasize positive achievements because, if achievements turn into negatives unexpectedly, they may cause embarrassment for the school, its staff, or the principal personally. We were told also that the teaching profession is not accustomed to a show-and-tell mentality or to overt promotion of its own achievements. And we were reminded that for almost 40 years, the message of the Coleman report (Coleman,1966)—that schools don't make a difference to children's life chances—has cast a pall over the teaching profession.

In our case studies of successful school reform, principals tended to regard modeling optimism for their school communities and encouraging teachers to do the same as a professional responsibility. We observed parallel leadership, involving teacher leaders and their principals, being used in diverse ways to generate a culture of success out of what were frequently modest achievements.

In one elementary school, a week-long project involved staff and students in analyzing the school's culture using these provocative questions:

What do we look like? What would we like to look like?

What do we feel like? What would we like to feel like?

What do we sound like? What would we like to sound like?

What do we smell like? What would we like to smell like?

What do we taste like? What would we like to taste like?

The exercise not only created a colorful depiction of the school but also sparked leadership action among a number of previously non-engaged teachers. With the impetus that the activity spawned, the character and ethos of the school changed in a relatively brief period. The school eventually declared itself a "green school" in recognition of its ecological value base.

In one high school, department heads assumed responsibility for identifying and celebrating student achievements that grew out of the school's agreed-on approach to teaching and learning. The department heads in question viewed themselves—and became widely regarded by others—as guardians of the school culture, a critical link between the teaching and the strategic functions of the school.

An emphasis on meaningful culture building can provide potential teacher leaders with concrete experience in transposing their personal values into artifacts and symbols that enhance the school's distinctiveness and identity. Principals who emphasize culture building and encourage teacher engagement in associated processes help teachers to view themselves as generators of new forms of meaning and as shapers of community values (see Table 4.1). In this way, powerful new forms of educational leadership can be tapped, and the image of teaching as a leading profession is enhanced.

Conclusions

If, as Katzenmeyer and Moller (1996) assert, teacher leadership is an idea whose time has come, then the implications for school principals are considerable. Principals will need to become accustomed to unfamiliar approaches to power sharing. They will need to internalize new understanding about relationships between school-based leadership and school outcomes. And they will need to acquire skills and expertise in nurturing both teacher leadership and parallel leadership.

In addressing these issues here, we have focused our effort on seven challenges that principals, in case studies of successful school reform, confronted and turned to educational advantage. What emerges is new understanding of how principals might encourage and nurture teacher leadership. But this understanding also extends to a new role for principals, one that is suited to the demands of school leadership in a knowledge-based society. It is a role that highlights the central importance of schoolwide approaches to pedagogy and emphasizes teaching as a leading profession. The new role it assigns principals is as exciting as teacher leadership is for teachers. It is a role that we believe principals everywhere will welcome.

We do not presume to have uncovered all the subtleties or complexities associated with teacher leadership, parallel leadership, and the principal's role in nurturing them both. But we believe we have un-

Table 4.1 Summary of the Principal's Role in Promoting Teacher Leadership

---

Communicate a clear strategic intent. Model futuristic thinking; provide a safe environment for exploration and experimentation; show the linking of visioning to knowledge creation.

Incorporate the aspirations and ideas of others. Demonstrate confidence in teachers' professional capabilities; help teachers clarify their personal values; explore the alignment between strategic and educational values.

Pose difficult-to-answer questions. Heighten the level of professional dialogue about educational practices; encourage individual commitment from alienated teachers.

Make space for individual innovation. Create opportunities for individual expression; encourage identification of—and confrontation of—institutional barriers.

Know when to step back. Demonstrate trust; illuminate how power can and should be distributed; acknowledge the importance of the individual professional; attest to the central place of teaching in school decision making.

Create opportunities out of perceived difficulties. Demonstrate ways in which knowledge may be created; encourage thinking outside the box.

Build on achievements to create a culture of success. Model positive problem solving; create an ethos of teachers as guardians of the school culture; demonstrate that from little acorns, big oak trees can grow.

---

covered sufficient material to demonstrate the essential meanings associated with these concepts and their extraordinary potential. That done, we now move to the second part of *Developing Teacher Leaders,* namely the action component.

PART 2

Developing Leaders

CHAPTER 5

Preparing for Teacher Leadership

How do we translate the leadership concepts presented in Part 1 into action in schools? This challenge is fundamental to our charge in writing this book. In composing the exercises in the next chapter, we sought to extend and deepen the meaning of the first premise of teacher leadership—that it exists, it is real. Because the best theories are the most practical, we knew we had to corroborate the second premise—that teacher leadership is grounded in educational theory. We also wanted to build on the third and fourth premises—teacher leadership is distinctive and diverse—by providing opportunities for teachers and administrators to develop and actualize their leadership capacities on site. Finally, we saw it as an inherent obligation to add proof to the fifth premise—teacher leadership can be nurtured and developed. So we designed a set of exercises that implant the seeds of teacher leadership and parallel leadership, foster their growth into seedlings, and, ultimately, guarantee their maturity as healthy trees rooted solidly in schools and communities.

The potential of teacher leadership and parallel leadership to assist with the revitalization of schools and the enhancement of the teaching profession is obvious. One needs to hear only bits of testimony from dedicated and competent professionals to feel this. A case in point is 2000 Michigan Teacher of the Year Margaret Holtschlag, who spoke (see interview in Appendix B) of an interchange she had the day she was honored, along with other state teachers of the year, at the White House in Washington:

I was having a conversation with one teacher who was fretting over not being worthy of being there that day—that there were so many others in her state that should be there instead of her. I pulled out my journal and read those six attributes of a teacher leader [in the Teachers as Leaders Framework, Table 1.1], and she and I talked about how those qualities of leadership make a difference in making our schools a better learning place for our students.

The ideas we sought to convey in Part 1 are the definition of teacher leadership, the Teachers as Leaders Framework, the definition of parallel leadership, how teacher leadership and parallel leadership interact to enhance school outcomes, and new roles for the principal. Threading through these ideas is the notion that school revitalization will not happen, and certainly will not be sustained, without teacher leadership. Yet there is also the understanding that teacher leadership, by itself, is not sufficient for school revitalization to occur and endure. Parallel leadership, enabled through new roles for principals, makes the leap from necessity to sufficiency possible. When teacher leaders are at work in their schools and communities—and teacher leaders and administrative leaders engage positively—the school and its students will succeed.

We developed exercises to enhance teachers' ability to become full partners in leadership necessary for an energized school. Although the exercises are aimed primarily at enhancing the leadership ability of teachers, administrators with whom teachers work must participate fully. The role of administrators in increasing leadership capacity in the school is critical. The exercises afford administrators a special opportunity not only to support emerging teacher leaders but also to enhance their own threshold for shared leadership.

Our research affirmed the worth and integrity of our ideas and prompted us to craft a full trial of them in the workplace. Thus in Part 2, we provide an opportunity for professionals to reinvent the ideas and apply them to their own schools. Through the exercises, concept and action come together, and teacher leadership and parallel leadership can be acted out and shaped into strategies that contribute to the education of children and youth.

Our objectives are simple and few. We want teachers and administrators to become conversant with the ideas in this book by experiencing them firsthand and adapting them for their own use. And we want to ensure that this opportunity is afforded them on safe ground during time set aside for professional development—in a space free of daily pressures from students, parents, and community.

Although teachers and administrators are the primary audience for the exercises, we believe that other groups interested in school revitalization can benefit from them—school improvement teams made up of teachers, administrators, parents, community leaders, and others; school boards or councils; other educational groups with a common set of goals—all can profit from the experiences in Part 2.

Our main intent, however, is to focus especially on leadership development needs of professionals working with one another in a school seeking to revitalize itself. The benefits of a professional learning community are established in the literature on successful school reform. We want to take advantage of the acceleration in learning that occurs when professionals come together and act as learning resources for each other.

Affirmation of the Developmental Approach Taken

Before introducing the exercises, we will cite the assumptions that guided our thinking. Recent concern about the quality of schooling in both the United States and Australia has produced a host of reform proposals. Most are measures directed specifically at how schools are governed and managed.

First, we believe that the development of market incentives through parental choice and charter schools, the widespread use of large-scale testing programs, and the imposition of subject matter standards and curriculum frameworks are the earmarks of present-day educational reform in the United States and, to some extent, in other countries, including Australia. Such measures have sidestepped a major undertaking that could make a difference in the quality of education—a significant investment in the development of teachers as professionals. Thus the strategy we recommend, expressed most tangibly in these exercises, is a human resource development strategy, thrust squarely against the prevailing political and organizational strategies of the day.

Second, almost all the exercises that follow fall into the category of formative or developmental experiences. They set the gears of teacher leadership in motion but do not take teachers and administrators far down the road of implementing specific initiatives in their schools. This limitation we readily accept, believing that teachers—and probably most other direct-service professionals—need to get their leadership feet under them before undertaking serious workplace initiatives. This is principally because teachers and their colleagues in other fields have been deprived of significant leadership development opportunities. The role of teacher, as traditionally defined, does not include the capabilities contained in the Teachers as Leaders Framework. Nor have contemporary reform measures encouraged development of teacher leaders. To the contrary, many have been hostile to teachers assuming leadership.

Therefore, we submit that effective leadership development requires aspiring leaders to go slow in order to go fast—to build a strong foundation before attempting in the workplace serious initiatives that touch children, youth, and their parents. Many promising and well-intentioned efforts to engage people as leaders have failed because necessary developmental steps, such as the ones represented in the exercises in the next chapter, are overlooked.

Third, the exercises are designed primarily for use by teachers and administrators. Development of mutually supportive leadership patterns between teachers and administrators can occur only if the two parties work together. Trust and mutual confidence must be established through systematic interaction.

Fourth and finally, we acknowledge legitimate concern about whether the leadership development strategy represented by the exercises really works. How can one be sure that the strategy implicit in the 14 exercises will produce the outcomes sought? The honest answer: No definitive proof exists that experiential leadership development yields greater leadership capacity. But plenty of anecdotal evidence suggests that the strategy powerfully affects how school professionals perform. The work of a host of organizational development consultants, including one of the authors, offers support here.

We are confident, in any event, that our approach is considerably more effective than are didactic approaches. If the users of the exercises can consciously make the leap from experience to concept formation and from concept formation to workplace application, then results can be telling. Our case rests in the power of reflective practice and constructivism—of professionals learning through experience in cooperation with other learners.

Key Facets of the Exercises

Two important aspects give shape to the exercises.

First, they are experiential in that they call on participants to engage in self-analysis, problem solving, or idea creation that relates directly or indirectly to their workplace challenges. The exercises are platforms that teachers and administrators can use to make meaning about their work with each other and with other key actors in the school and community. Consonant with the definition of teacher leadership, which involves the power of teaching to shape meaning, these exercises enhance the capacity of teachers to do that for themselves.

Some of the exercises call on participants to wrestle with issues that are at the heart of their school leadership responsibilities. Selected exercises spotlight the use of leadership language in the school (The Power of Language), teachers' diverse educational approaches and beliefs (Spots), and the relationship of daily actions to school vision (Lights! Action!). Other exercises invite participants to engage in simulations that bear on leadership capacity in general but are not directly related to teacher leadership or parallel leadership per se. You will find exercises dealing with how potential leaders should view past mistakes (Oops!) or deal with the complex dynamics of prior professional relationships (The Past). Yet other exercises are metaphor-making opportunities that allow participants to frame complex ideas in novel ways or to identify common ground as a basis for collective effort. Examples include participants' perspectives on the state of parallel leadership in their school (Parallel Scenarios) and directions they might pursue through their newly developed leadership capacity (Imagine!).

Regardless of medium or mode, all the exercises promote inductive thinking. They encourage teachers and administrators to construct their own meaning about themselves and their environment, to form their own interpretation of what is possible and of what stands in their way, and to understand what they themselves bring in terms of both possibility and disability. With adequate facilitation, the exercises can move participants to reflect—individually and collectively—on their job responsibilities, through experiences that are related directly or indirectly to the school. From these reflections, they can determine their own leadership agenda and begin to act on it.

Second, the demands that the exercises place on participants are, for the most part, beyond the frame of their day-to-day responsibilities. Out of the path of the normally high-stakes atmosphere of classroom teaching, the exercises can engender a sense of openness and freedom and a spirit of experimentation. Although the content of some of the exercises approximates existing school challenges, several are somewhat distant. The combination of the two is intentional. The latter allow participants to step away from the more gripping and immediate problems confronting them. They offer an opportunity, through simulation, for participants to wrestle with generic challenges inherent in leadership. The former pull participants back to their daily responsibilities, but their focus is on schoolwide problems, not classroom-specific issues. All in all, we regard the exercises as a diverse mix of relevant and compelling challenges, aimed at helping teachers and administrators work together to revitalize their school. Every professional development program should contain this level of diversity and richness so that real and sustainable growth can occur.

The Matter of Values

The exercises are platforms only. They set the stage for substantive direction setting by participants but do not prescribe particular directions. Yet inherent in them are explicit values. In particular, they foster greater common understanding among professionals, encourage collegial trust and respect, and spur joint action. Through collaborative decision making and joint determination of priority tasks, they advance the idea that professionals who share the same concerns can exert significant influence over the character of their work environments. The message in the exercises is clear: that individuals working together can overcome barriers and get essential work done. While leaving direction setting to the participants, the exercises, nonetheless, compel attention to issues of teaching, learning, and assessment—the special focus of teacher leadership.

Bolman and Deal (1994) lend credence to the kind of leadership development that the exercises support. Summarizing the work of a distinguished panel on education leadership development, they highlight several desirable dimensions of more effective programs. Principal among them are the ideas that "leadership is cultivated or nurtured primarily through experience" (p. 87) and that "reflection and dialogue with others help people to learn to lead" (p. 88). The exercises in Part 2 are directly responsive to these guidelines.

Echoing the voice of others, such as Clark and Clark (1994) of the Center for Creative Leadership, Bolman and Deal (1994) insist that "leadership can be taught—but not the way we currently do it" (p. 92). They argue that human and spiritual dimensions must play a greater part, and they stress the role of values in leadership development: "Programs will need to reinforce in potential leaders the importance of values, symbols, and symbolic exercise and how these can be shaped and encouraged to give meaning and purpose to collective endeavors" (p. 93).

The exercises represent a significant opportunity for teachers and administrators to step away from what they do in the course of a work day and add greater meaning, purpose, and effect to their professional roles. Specifically, the exercises invite teachers and administrators to ask the following:

- What does taking educational leadership mean for us?

- What would taking leadership look like, feel like, sound like?

- How should teacher leadership intersect that of the principal and other administrators?

- Ultimately, how can we do our part in fulfilling educational leadership responsibilities on behalf of the children and youth we serve?

Caveats

Several caveats apply as professionals undertake a self-development project composed largely of experiential exercises. Included are the following:

- Acceptance by participants of the responsibilities inherent in their ownership of the outcomes of the exercises

- Acceptance of the impact of this kind of professional development on relationships within the school

- The need for administrator understanding, endorsement, and support

- The need to keep all affected constituents informed of progress

- The requirement that participants be familiar with the ideas in Part 1, especially the relationship of schoolwide pedagogy to enhanced outcomes

- A willingness to secure an able and trusted facilitator to assist with the exercises

Ownership

Participants, and participants alone, own the yield of the exercises. Simply said, the exercises promote individual and collective understanding, the identification of participants' aspirations, and the shaping of their perspectives on professional roles and responsibilities. They are not meant to comprise an inservice training workshop as commonly understood, where intended outcomes are imposed, to a greater or lesser extent, on the teaching staff.

With ownership of the yield of the exercises comes significant responsibility—active participation on the part of all, for instance. The guidelines for participants are that they operate as equals and throw themselves like seeds into all the activities and follow-up discussions. The image of self-empowered embryos is on the mark here. Participants should do their best to engage reflectively and self-critically in these uncomplicated, low-stakes activities and discussions, which reflect actual experience but are removed from participants' real work in classrooms. They are uncomplicated because they skirt many of the complexities of existing work relationships, and they are low stakes because children, youth, and board or council members are not present. From wholehearted and full participation comes the potential for new ideas and attitudes and the possibility of substantial growth and development.

Impact

Although some of the exercises may bear only an indirect relationship to the work of the school, their impact on school policies and professional relationships will likely be substantial. After all, organizational relationships hinge on values and inclinations. As participants' values and inclinations shift in the wake of their shared experiences, the balance of power among them will shift as well. Participants should, therefore, approach the exercises soberly, understanding that their perspective may be transformed after working through the exercises with their colleagues.

Adjustments of formal and informal relationships may disturb delicate balances that have existed in the school for a considerable period. Care and compassion for one's colleagues should prevail, and a concern for the welfare of students should be the main touchstone for all activities and discussions.

Need for Self-Assessment

The exercises are a beginning for participants who envision the promise of teacher leadership and parallel leadership for their school and the students it serves. But the exercises should not be construed as forming a comprehensive program for installing teacher leadership in a school. Before undertaking the exercises, potential users should ask themselves whether they delved into the core concepts of teacher leadership and parallel leadership presented in Part 1. They should assess carefully whether the values underlying parallel leadership, as discussed in Chapter 3, apply in their workplace. These values include mutual respect, a sense of shared purpose, and allowance for individual expression. Potential users should also inspect the definitions of teacher leadership and parallel leadership in Chapters 1 and 3 respectively and ask themselves whether they perceive the potential in themselves and in their school and community to accept new kinds of leadership. They should examine the Teachers as Leaders Framework and reflect on the extent to which some of the elements in the Framework are already present in the work of the teaching staff. In summary, participants should look inside themselves to see if they really agree with the assumption underlying this book—that increasing a school's leadership capacity will help it do a better job of educating students.

A propitious time to begin a substantial leadership development effort is the point at which a school undertakes a major school improvement effort. Perhaps the principal, district level administrators, or state officials are under pressure to improve student outcomes, and they suspect that relationships in the school must change if it is to respond positively. Perhaps the school staff itself wants to collaborate on teaching approaches or better use learning resources outside the school. In sum, when concerns about the quality of teaching and learning in the school are front and center, the receptivity to teacher leadership is likely to be greatest.

Necessary Facilitation

To attain the most positive effects from these exercises, a facilitator should be appointed to assist the group, preferably a respected colleague with background in organizational development and skill in facilitating sensitive group discussions. Whether an insider or an outsider, the facilitator should be familiar with the core concepts presented in Part 1 before commencing the professional learning and development process outlined in the next chapter.

It is possible to achieve creditable results with an insider who shares the confidence of the group yet has enough independence to be of service to it. But there are marked advantages to having an outside facilitator. Two of the most notable advantages are (a) the added perspective and expertise and (b) the sense of accountability that the presence of an outsider nearly always imposes on participants. Although it is understood that there are advantages to outside facilitation, for purposes of clarity and ease, the exercises are written as if teachers and administrators themselves will carry them out and discuss the results and implications using one of their number as facilitator.

Almost all the learning from the exercises derives from the discussions that follow the activities, not from the activities themselves. The participants, with the facilitator's help, engage in dialogue after an activity—to understand what happened, what the implications are of what happened, and what the potential applications are to the work of the school staff. The discussion following an activity is the point of discernible impact for the time spent in an activity. Participants can assess in the discussion what they have gleaned from the more artificial world of the activity and how the learning from it can be insinuated into their real work world.

Specific tasks are described more fully in Chapter 6. For now, here is an overview of functions performed by the facilitator:

- Conduct an orientation for each session, inviting the group to review implications, reflections, and proposed actions from the previous session and to establish desired outcomes for the exercise at hand

- Set up and lead each exercise with the group, and observe the progress of the group in terms of

    content and quality of interactions among participants

    emergence of shared understanding on certain points among group members

    decision-making dynamics

    framing of leadership concepts

    extent of individual and group self-confidence regarding capacity to affect important educational functions in the school and beyond

- Pose a series of questions to the group to debrief them after each exercise, allowing responses of participants to guide the dialogue. (Suggested discussion questions are listed within each exercise description.)

- Document the outcome of the group's work, including the major outcomes of each exercise and the overall effect of the sequence of exercises

Sequence and Cumulative Effect

The exercises are sequenced to provide cumulative impact. Spots, for example, is likely to be more successful if it follows Readiness than if it precedes it. Therefore, we strongly suggest that participants adhere as closely as possible to the sequence in which the exercises appear in Chapter 6.

After an initial exercise that allows participants to see for themselves the leadership talent in the room, participants assess their readiness for new forms of leadership and grapple with issues fundamental to taking leadership regardless of context. With this initial grounding, participants undertake the difficult task of building a foundation for significant teacher leadership and parallel leadership initiatives. They then move on, in the final exercises, to mapping future endeavors and testing their mettle on a specific challenge that confronts every school staff.

The first exercise is a warm up called Group Portrait. From it, participants learn about the leadership assets of the group, including relevant aspects of members' backgrounds and the special talents each brings to the work they will share. The Readiness exercise provides participants with a quick and easy assessment of their individual and collective fitness and willingness to undertake teacher leadership initiatives.

The intent of the two experiences that follow is to raise participants' consciousness of both the promise inherent in leadership and leadership's persistent challenges. Understanding the inevitability of making mistakes and the value of reflection in fostering organizational innovation are the themes in Oops. The impact of effective interaction among coworkers on the quality of collective output is the main thrust of Creative Tension. The Power of Language, the final exercise in this set, serves as a complement to Readiness in that it offers participants an opportunity to analyze the leadership language that school staff members use on a regular basis. This is an important indicator of the degree of openness to increased leadership density within the school.

The assumption underlying these preliminary exercises is that professionals contemplating new forms of leadership need to experience the struggles involved and decide whether they have the wherewithal to overcome obstacles. The dynamics of coming to terms with one's mistakes and of engaging in vigorous interactions with one's colleagues are elemental but necessary first steps for those intending to energize their schools and raise their own status as professionals.

With an initial grip on selected leadership dynamics and on the group's readiness and capacity to engage in school revitalization initiatives, the participants then begin to put in place a set of building blocks that equip them for action. Spots serves as a bridge between exercises just completed and those about to be experienced. From the exercise, participants gain baseline knowledge of where their colleagues stand on issues of teaching and learning in the school. Participants are invited, in the next exercise, The Past, to put prior working relationships into perspective and move on to a more fruitful future. Barriers, which follows, provides an inventory of the encumbrances that participants perceive as standing in the way of initiatives they might undertake together. It also beckons participants to chart paths through or around identified barriers. The concluding experience in this set, Assumptions, helps participants see how their initial conceptions stack up against a theoretical framework of ideas about teacher leadership and parallel leadership drawn from the literature.

Parallel Scenarios, the first exercise in the last set, explores the forms that parallel leadership has taken and might take in the school. Imagine!, the next exercise, asks participants to determine a shared vision of teacher leadership and parallel leadership, and to become more explicit about individual and group values. From Lights! Action!, participants frame actions that track with the school's declared vision. Staff Meeting provides a tangible testing ground for participants' capacity and will, stemming from earlier developmental work. Although still in a formative stage, the group is ready to effect shared leadership in the school as professional equals capable of contributing to school revitalization. The last exercise, Six Months Later and Beyond, offers an opportunity to track the unfolding of the school's new approach to leadership.

Expected Outcomes

Participants can expect these outcomes from the effort invested in this developmental sequence of exercises:

- Deepened commitment of all staff members to an achievable school vision and to preliminary ground work for aligning the school's vision and teaching practices schoolwide

- Greater understanding by teachers of the political and organizational challenges the administrators face

- Greater understanding by administrators of the multiple and interrelated forms of leadership required to improve teaching practices

- Greater understanding by all staff members of the multiple and interrelated forms of leadership required to gain community support for the school

- The identification of new initiatives leading to schoolwide approaches to pedagogy and, ultimately, improved student outcomes

- More collaborative, less hierarchical, teacher-administrator relationships

- Teacher-driven professional development

- Staff meetings that are more purposive and are characterized by more productive interchanges

Through the exercises, participants can produce a *leadership portfolio* that will advance their future leadership endeavors. In the portfolio will be a number of instruments for fashioning a schoolwide approach to teaching, learning, and assessment. The portfolio can be expanded as teachers add to their leadership repertoire. The instruments in it can be sharpened as teachers become more adept at the leadership they undertake. The portfolio includes the following:

- A grid that depicts the use of leadership language in the school (see Exercise 5)

- A delineation of the barriers that stand in the way of teacher leadership (see Exercise 8)

- A written set of assumptions about leadership in the school (see Exercise 9)

- A visual metaphor depicting the promise of teacher leadership and parallel leadership in the school (see Exercise 10)

- An analysis of the alignment of daily actions with the school's vision or mission (see Exercise 11)

- A proposed revamping of the school's staff meeting (see Exercise 13)

Conclusions

The exercises in the next chapter are a significant and practical complement to the ideas in the preceding chapters. At the heart of the definition of teacher leadership in Chapter 1 is the power of teaching to assist
others in shaping meaning. These exercises are a fit application of that
definition, because they provide an opportunity for teachers themselves to shape what it means to take leadership in their schools on behalf of the children and youth they serve.

Undertaken with openness, earnestness, and diligence, the exercises can, we believe, undergird potent school reform and enhancement of the professional status of teachers. To accomplish these ambitious aims, potential participants need to embark on this professional
development opportunity fully aware of the concepts on which they are
based and on the conditions that must be present in their schools for
the ideas to have a fair trial. They must, in effect, be intimately familiar
with the ideas in Part 1.

The exercises can promote growth and development that exceed
that which is usually attainable by reading ideas or even by discussing
them with colleagues. But participants must arrive at the doorstep of
these experiences fully committed to engage actively with the challenges they present and willing to push the limits of their own thinking
far beyond its current boundaries. Equipped with such attitudes and
supported by able facilitation, participants can be confident that the
simulations, self-assessments, and metaphor-making opportunities in
these exercises will have the desired effect.

CHAPTER 6

The Exercises

List of Exercises by Purpose

Cultivating Leadership Consciousness and Gauging Readiness

- **Group Portrait.** Learn about colleagues' leadership assets.

- **Readiness.** Establish participants' readiness for teacher leadership.

- **Oops!** Focus on risk taking as a fundamental requirement for organizational innovation.

- **Creative Tension.** Feel how the push and pull of vigorous interaction produces positive results.

- **The Power of Language.** Examine how the language that staff members use promotes or inhibits the potential for teacher leadership and parallel leadership.

Building a Base for Schoolwide Leadership

- **Spots.** Identify participants' diverse perspectives on a teaching and learning challenge they face together, and foster a concerted response.

- **The Past.** Place the encumbering aspects of the past in perspective to make room for future productivity.

- **Barriers.** Explore the elements that stand in the way of emergent teacher leadership.

- **Assumptions.** Uncover ways of thinking that affect actions and determine possibilities for teacher leadership.

Actualizing Teacher Leadership for Successful School Revitalization

- **Parallel Scenarios.** Explore forms that parallel leadership has taken and might take in the school.

- **Imagine!** Create a visual image of teacher leadership and parallel leadership in the school.

- **Lights! Action!** Identify, examine, and assess actions that support the school's vision.

- **Staff Meeting.** Demonstrate how teacher leadership can invigorate one of the school's essential functions.

- **Six Months Later and Beyond.** Reflect on the impact of leadership development efforts on school improvement and enhanced student outcomes.

Exercises for Cultivating Leadership Consciousness and Gauging Readiness

Exercise 1: Group Portrait

Purpose. This exercise acquaints participants with each other's views, strengths, and values—and provides an initial basis for trusting professional relationships.

Rationale. The experiences and views of group members are significant resources for undertaking leadership initiatives. They are, in effect, the raw material of the group's leadership capacity. When mustered and energized, these resources comprise a group's power to move forward and get things done. Therefore, a group has to become as well informed as possible about each other's views, strengths, and values. And its members have to think about how to translate these assets into achievement of common goals. When this process of becoming acquainted takes place with care and respect, then trust, the basis of all positive action in organizations, can be built.

Time Considerations and Necessary Materials. The exercise is meant to unfold in more than one session. In total, the experience should consume anywhere from 1 to 3 hours, depending on how much depth participants seek to achieve. We recommend that participants address the questions below, perhaps adding a similar question or two of their own. An overhead projector and transparencies that can be written on are the only necessary materials.

Process

→ Participants stand or sit in a circle or at least position themselves so that everyone can see each other. The facilitator notes that she or he is going to ask a series of questions to which all will respond. Participants should listen carefully to their colleagues' responses, because after the questions are asked and answered, they will synthesize the data presented, in order to compose a group portrait based on the collective responses to the questions. As an inducement to careful listening, participants may want to don blindfolds for the question and response period, at least for the first group of questions. Rather than going around the circle in one direction, participants might spontaneously volunteer answers to the questions until all have had an opportunity to do so.

→ Possible questions are listed below. Group size will determine the number and nature of questions and whether a response from every person on every question is necessary. Useful questions are ones that uncover participants' origins; tastes; inclinations; and views about teaching, learning, social justice, and leadership. At this stage of group development, it is important that questioning be focused yet gentle. Group members should take care to preserve as much privacy as the most sensitive person in the group needs and to be careful about seeking disclosure from group members prematurely.

- Where did your inspiration to teach come from?

- Where and when did you learn the most about how to teach?

- Where and when did you learn the most about how kids learn?

- Where and when did you learn the most about how adults learn?

- What's the best professional-renewal experience you, as an adult professional, ever had?

- When you're not teaching, what do you do for personal renewal?

- What was the most egregious instance of unfair treatment you observed in an educational setting? How and how well was that instance dealt with?

- Where and when did you learn the most about leadership?

- Cite one example of superb educational leadership, and explain how it affected you?

- When you think of teacher leadership as outlined in the Teachers as Leaders Framework (Table 1.1), what person, situation, or event immediately comes to mind?

As responses are offered, the facilitator and other participants may probe a little to have their colleagues articulate values behind responses. For example, the second question above could be followed with, "Why was this significant for you?" "How does that relate to what you consider important in teaching?" Include, if you wish, in the discussion around the fourth question, "How did you learn this?" "What was it about leadership that struck a chord with you?" In discussing the last question, you may want to ask, "Which elements of the framework were most easily identifiable?" "What made this situation an example of leadership rather than one of good teaching?"

→ After participants address each set of questions in small groups, the group as a whole engages in a discussion that addresses the following questions:

- What are our general observations about the character of this group?

- Are we a heterogeneous or homogeneous group? In what ways? What strengths or limitations does this imply for us?

- Are there shared or common points of view in the way we think about learning? About fairness? About leadership? About diverse points of view?

- What is the group's understanding of, and attitude toward, teacher leadership?

➔ (If the group is small enough, the following activity may be undertaken by all participants working together. If the group is large, one or two participants could volunteer to work on it after the session and present it to the group at its next meeting.) Based on the question and answer sessions and the subsequent debriefings, compose a verbal portrait of the group, including as many descriptors as possible. Descriptors should summarize group characteristics and pinpoint strengths and weaknesses. The portrait should be as honest and forthright as possible. The facilitator might add other observations to give this initial portrait additional richness, contour, and color. Someone then writes the group portrait on a transparency so that everyone can discuss it. The aim of the discussion is to test for accuracy and fullness of description, not to water down differences or artificially build common ground.

➔ As participants conclude this exercise, they should record in their journals at least one significant observation drawn from the discussions. They might also make note of a person who has a markedly different viewpoint from their own about an aspect of teaching or leadership, and undertake to engage in a professional conversation on the topic with that person during the following week.

Exercise 2: Readiness

Purpose. This activity provides an indication of participants' individual and collective perceptions of leadership and their readiness for teacher leadership and parallel leadership.

Rationale. Self-knowledge is critical to the development of teacher leadership. It is essential for a group considering leadership initiatives to determine how much agreement there is in the room about the dimensions and dynamics of leadership. It is equally important for the group to be clear about differences of view. Through Readiness, group members build this picture of similarities and disparities from the ground up, from pairs to foursomes to the group as a whole.

Time Considerations and Necessary Materials. Completing the self-survey should take participants only 30 minutes. The exercise itself will likely consume about 1½ to 2 hours. Necessary materials include an overhead projector and transparencies that can be written on, writing materials, a flipchart and markers, completed self-surveys, and the scoring protocol.

Self Survey to Assess Readiness for Leadership

Figure 6.1 is a self-survey for each member of the group to complete individually.

Scoring Protocol for the Self-Survey

1. Count the number of times you chose *strongly disagree.*

   Multiply by –2, and write the number here: _____

2. Count the number of times you chose *disagree.*

   Multiply by –1, and write the number here: _____

3. Ignore the number of times you chose *no opinion.*

4. Count the number of times you chose *agree.*

   Write the number here: _____

5. Count the number of times you chose *strongly agree.*

   Multiply by 2, and write the number here: _____

6. Write the total of these 4 numbers here: _____

If the number on line 6 is between 21 and 30:

   Virtually all your attitudes, values, and beliefs align with the tenets of teacher leadership and parallel leadership.

If the number on line 6 is between 11 and 20:

   The majority of your attitudes, values, and beliefs align with the tenets of teacher leadership and parallel leadership.

If the number on line 6 is between 1 and 10:

   Some of your attitudes, values, and beliefs align with the tenets of teacher leadership and parallel leadership. Several don't.

If the number on line 6 is less than 1:

   Few of your attitudes, values, and beliefs align with the tenets of teacher leadership and parallel leadership.

Figure 6.1. Self-Survey

Respond to the Statements Below	Strongly Disagree	Disagree	No Opinion	Agree	Strongly Agree
Teaching is as important as any other profession.	≤	≤	≤	≤	≤
Part of being a teacher is influencing the educational ideas of other teachers, administrators, parents, and community leaders.	≤	≤	≤	≤	≤
Teachers should be recognized for trying new teaching strategies whether or not they succeed.	≤	≤	≤	≤	≤
Teachers should participate actively in educational policy making.	≤	≤	≤	≤	≤
Good teaching involves observing, and providing feedback to, fellow teachers.	≤	≤	≤	≤	≤
Administrators are a potential source of facilitative assistance for teachers.	≤	≤	≤	≤	≤
Teachers are responsible for encouraging a schoolwide approach to teaching, learning, and assessment.	≤	≤	≤	≤	≤
Teachers can continue with classroom instruction and, at the same time, be a school leader.	≤	≤	≤	≤	≤

continued

Figure 6.1. Continued

Respond to the Statements Below	Strongly Disagree	Disagree	No Opinion	Agree	Strongly Agree
Teachers should allocate time to help plan schoolwide professional development activities.	≤	≤	≤	≤	≤
Teachers should know how organizations work and be effective at getting things done in them.	≤	≤	≤	≤	≤
Mentoring new teachers is part of the professional responsibility of a teacher.	≤	≤	≤	≤	≤
An active role in decision making about instructional materials, allocation of learning resources, and student assignments is one of a teacher's responsibilities.	≤	≤	≤	≤	≤
An educational leader should convey optimism to students, colleagues, and parents.	≤	≤	≤	≤	≤
Teaching means standing up for all students, including those who are marginalized and disadvantaged.	≤	≤	≤	≤	≤
Teachers have knowledge and skills that can help their fellow teachers succeed with students, and these should be incorporated in professional development efforts.	≤	≤	≤	≤	≤

Source: Adapted from a questionnaire created by Katzenmeyer and Moller (1996) and grounded in the six elements in the Teachers as Leaders Framework.

Process

➜ Participants write their own definition of leadership in a paragraph and then condense it into a simple phrase and, finally, into one word, if possible.

➜ Then participants seek out the person in the room they know the least. These pairs discuss their own personal [i.e., not the self-survey] definitions, identify the common ground between them, and note key differences.

➜ Now the established pairs join with another pair and, as a group of four, they repeat the process. Group members identify common ground and note key differences.

➜ The groups of four report their findings to the entire group and include a short summary of the process they used to determine similarities and differences.

➜ Using these responses as a catalyst, participants discuss the extent of common understanding of leadership and the diverse points of view within the group. They write these on transparencies for the entire group to ponder and deliberate.

➜ It is now time for participants to reflect on the self-survey results, focusing first on the average score for the group as a whole. This score offers a simple picture of the group's collective readiness for teacher leadership and parallel leadership.

Note of Caution. The score may signal the need to decide on how to proceed with the remainder of the leadership development exercises in this chapter. If the average score indicates a strong or moderate readiness for teacher leadership (over 11), then the group should feel confident in proceeding with the remaining exercises, using only a colleague for facilitation. If the average score is less than 11, and the group wants to proceed, then we recommend that they engage an outside facilitator who is an expert in organizational development.

➜ Discussion among participants now focuses on the compiled results. For example, the group takes a closer look at those items on the survey that were marked *agree* or *strongly agree* on a number of the completed surveys. Do participants, in fact, take actions consonant with these positions of agreement? If not, do they believe action is warranted? If they do not currently act on them, how could they take the lead in fulfilling one or more? The facilitator might identify one item as a case in point (say, observing and providing feedback to fellow teachers, item #5 in Figure 6.1), and the group could brainstorm about specific steps they can take to do this better, and record the steps on the flipchart.

➜ Participants then form into the groups of four that they worked in previously, and each group identifies one initiative, related to the survey items, on which they wish to work and take a lead role in the school. As expeditiously as possible, the groups move from free-flowing generation of ideas to laying out specific actions they are willing to take to enhance their readiness for leadership.

➜ Then, as a whole group, they review the results of the small-group sessions and seek agreement on three or four key actions that they, either as a whole group or in subgroups, will undertake in a meaningful and practical way.

➜ The whole group, with the aid of the facilitator, composes a summary picture (graphically and verbally) of what it has agreed to do and keeps this as a representation of the group's intentions.

A Final Note. Through this exercise, participants should form a clearer understanding of their collective thinking about leadership, including points of agreement and disagreement within the group. They should also generate ideas on how to take advantage of potential leadership opportunities and, finally, should identify initiatives that may assist in this respect. Teacher leaders should acknowledge that they will face difficult dilemmas as they assume leadership responsibilities. Several of these may come to the surface in the course of doing this exercise. Additional time might well be allocated for the whole group to discuss potential dilemmas, how they might have already manifested themselves in the functioning of the school, and how they can best be addressed. Participants can be confident, however, that succeeding exercises will provide more opportunities for discussions along similar lines.

Exercise 3: Oops!

Purpose. This exercise promotes the realization that making mistakes is an inevitable outgrowth of risk taking, yet risk taking is essential for organizational innovation.

Rationale. All forms of leadership involve interactions among people and begin, for the most, part in individual risk taking—"going out on a limb," "cutting against the grain," "swimming against the tide." Teacher leadership and parallel leadership are no different from other kinds of leadership. Assuredly, actions that fit within the context of the Teachers as Leaders Framework require substantial risk taking. One person with an idea about which she is convinced steps forward, conveys that idea to her peers, seeks to persuade them of its merits, and asks for their support. Then she, and perhaps they, try it out. People who make these sorts of moves inevitably make mistakes. The extent of support for making mistakes is the extent to which the group or organization will innovate. How a group or organization deals with mistake making fosters or detracts from its fledgling leadership capacity.

To assume leadership, individuals must first look within and find the resources to support their risk taking, to oil their springs of action. This exercise provides lubrication for the springs of action by inviting participants to build a network of support for making mistakes, for failing to meet their own performance expectations or those of others. The exercise helps participants see that perceived shortfalls have, in large part, led to their greatest learning and then to subsequent successes. An appreciation of the role of failure, the risk taking that leads up to it, the learning that takes place in its wake, and, ultimately, the potential for understanding and support from one's colleagues—these are fundamental to increasing leadership capacity.

Important Note. The exercise requires a level of professional and personal trust among participants, akin to the level of trust they will need to undertake leadership initiatives together. So, for some, the exercise might be a stretch, especially because it is early in the sequence exercises. Yet we believe the potential benefits outweigh the potential risks here, and participants should take the leap of faith that the exercise calls for.

Time Considerations and Necessary Materials. The exercise can be done in 1 hour. Needed are an overhead projector with blank transparencies that can be written on and a flipchart with markers.

Process

➡ Participants break into groups of three, and each person follows this prompt:

Think of a time when you went out on a limb for what you believed was an educationally defensible position. In so doing, you created unforeseen negative effects. Yet your stance proved to be an important learning experience for you. Describe the situation and the way apparent negatives led to some positive outcomes.

➡ When participants have identified at least one such instance, they describe it to their two colleagues, and then all three discuss its key aspects in terms of the nature of the incident, the extent of its effects, and the unanticipated positive consequences.

➡ After about 10 minutes of discussion in the groups of three, all join in a whole-group discussion. Participants offer some of their own stories and also contribute summary comments from their small groups.

➡ Then the whole group works toward formulating tentative conclusions based in themes common to the individual stories and to the small group's comments on them. The following questions may be used to guide the discussion:

- What were the common themes or elements among the experiences?

- What do these stories tell us about learning?

- What light do the stories shed on what it means to be a leader? What do they say about the relationship among making mistakes, risk taking, and leadership?

- Do the stories, taken together, tell us anything about teacher leadership?

- Refer, for example, to the snapshots in Part 1 and discuss how you believe that the teachers in them dealt with the continuum from making mistakes to taking leadership.

- What will you do to ensure that the lessons, whatever they are for you, are applied as you undertake serious work with each other and with other school and community leaders?

➡ To bring the activity to a close, participants jot a reflection in their journals, highlighting some of the most significant learning for them from today's session.

Exercise 4: Creative Tension

Purpose. This simulation invites participants to explore the tension between individual action and collaboration, and how this tension relates to the exercise of leadership.

Rationale. Leadership originates in the leader's mind and heart, and plays out in relationships with those whose minds and hearts the leader influences. Inevitably, a leadership dynamic involves at least two people trying to achieve a common end. Teacher leadership beckons teachers to reach beyond their work in the classroom and form relationships with other teachers to improve schoolwide processes. Thus increased understanding of the dynamics involved in striving for a common goal is essential for emergent teacher leaders.

Both the challenges and consequences of taking initiative interactively are illuminated through this series of simple floor maneuvers. Although the exercise is mild in its physical demands, the group, by itself or with the aid of its facilitator, should make accommodations to keep all participants safe.

Important Note. People uncomfortable with the physical nature of this activity should be urged to proceed cautiously and, if necessary, take an alternative approach to participation. Rather than undertaking the activity directly, they should position themselves to the side of colleagues who are faced off and ready to proceed. As these colleagues undertake the physical challenge, those on the side should gently place their hands on the arms of engaged participants and feel the dynamics of the activity without disrupting its flow.

There is power in the metaphor that this exercise presents. Participants should be active, physically and mentally, whether they are direct or indirect participants. The challenge for direct participants is to move from a sitting position to being up on their feet, and to do this gracefully and synchronously; indirect participants should notice the unfolding dynamics of this maneuver. Similar dynamics will come into play, to one extent or another, as participants work to bring the benefits of teacher leadership and parallel leadership to their school.

Time Considerations and Necessary Materials. The exercise, including the discussion that follows the activity, should take about an hour. Needed are enough floor space, free of tables and chairs, for participants to perform the exercise in twos, in small groups, and then as a whole group.

Process

➜ Direct participants sit on the floor, knees half bent, arms resting on their knees. They test to see if they can move easily from this position into a standing position without any physical contact with another person and without pushing down on the floor with their hands. Indirect participants observe. After one or two tries at this, some are accomplishing the move with ease, others with difficulty, and some are not able to do it at all.

➜ Direct participants then break into pairs and sit on the floor facing each other in close proximity, knees half bent, able to reach out and clasp each other's hands while arms rest on knees. Next, partners join forces to see if they can hoist each other from sitting to standing positions. The aim is to accomplish this gracefully and synchronously. The two can position their feet and knees as they choose and join hands and arms at will. Indirect participants stand beside the pair and place their hands on the joined arms as the direct participants perform the action.

➜ After a couple of attempts by the pairs to stand up, participants form groups of four to six and sit, as before, on the floor, facing each other in a circle. These groups have the same challenge as the pairs—to hoist themselves from a sitting to a standing position, working together gracefully and synchronously. The groups should discuss strategy before attempting a joint move. Indirect participants join the discussion and do as they did before, when the participants engage in the maneuver.

➜ After the small groups have made a few attempts at hoisting themselves to standing positions, the entire group, however large, forms a circle and sees if they can gracefully and synchronously get all members from their initial sitting positions to standing positions. As before, participants can position their feet, legs, hands, and arms however they choose. Again, a group discussion prior to execution is desirable. Indirect participants join in the discussion and perform hands-on observation during the physical maneuver.

Discussion in the wake of the activity should center on the following questions:

- There were four different ways you went about accomplishing the goal of standing up—singly, in pairs, as a small group, and as a whole group. What were the differences and similarities among them?

- What do you gather from this exercise about the dynamics of figuring out a solution to a problem by yourself and effecting it? About the dynamics of working in pairs? Working as a small group? As a large group?

- Are there lessons here for how members of groups might work more effectively with each other?

- Remembering the six elements in the Teachers as Leaders Framework, consider how each might involve creative tension between individual action and collaboration?

Exercise 5: The Power of Language

Purpose. Participants inquire into the language of leadership now in use in the school.

Rationale. How people speak about each other in the course of their work together, even when they use humor or tease, can be indicative of what they value more and what they value less. Shared leadership, in general, depends on factors such as trust, integrity, and good will. Parallel leadership, in particular, depends on mutual respect and regard, a sense of shared purpose, and allowance for individual expression. By assessing the leadership language used in a school, participants can learn for themselves the extent to which the school culture is amenable to teacher leadership, and whether it is, in fact, a place where parallel leadership has a chance to take hold and thrive.

Two challenges in this exercise are (a) to avoid intense personal reactions to certain words and expressions, and (b) to resist generalizing about how negative a word or expression is. For example, the use of *boss* may carry negative connotations in one situation but not in another, for one person but not another. These differences need to be explored, and participants should dig as deeply as they can into their consciousness to identify both positive and negative phrases and terms so that they can have a rich, full discussion of the implications for professional relationships and school culture.

Time Considerations and Necessary Materials. The exercise has three parts: (a) an initial discussion, (b) follow-up observations during the course of a week or two, and (c) a synthesizing discussion. Each discussion is likely to take over an hour, and intervening observations an hour as well. Necessary materials include an overhead projector, with transparencies

Table 6.1 Typical Expressions Associated With Four Leadership
Theories

Transformational leadership	"We are champions." "Climb every mountain." "Dream the impossible dream."
Strategic leadership	"The buck stops here." "If you can't beat them in the alleys, you can beat them on the playing field." "Results are all that count."
Educative or advocacy leadership	"Keep the scoundrels honest." "I'm an instigator." "Against all odds."
Organization-wide leadership	"We're a family." "We're all in this together." "A champion team will beat a team of champions."

that can be written on, and the Teachers as Leaders Framework enlarged
to poster size.

Process

→ Participants begin by sharing perspectives on the power of language—how it is used to achieve certain ends. Participants provide examples of ways they themselves have used language as a tool, considering both *what* was said and *how* it was said—and the power of both what and how to affect relationships.

→ Referring to the list of phrases associated with four traditional leadership theories (Table 6.1), participants discuss, as a group, their reactions to these phrases.

→ They then brainstorm about possible types of language used among school staff members in the normal course of their school day—for example, hierarchical, encouraging, aggressive, submissive, patronizing, inclusive, alienating, inspirational, confrontational. One member of the group writes the identified headings at the top of a flipchart page. Participants then form groups of three and discuss the words, phrases, and expressions that might fit under the headings just suggested.

➔ The small groups come together and share what they have written, so they can compile a comprehensive, varied collection of words, phrases, and expressions under appropriate headings. Participants ask various contributors to explain the context in which their word or phrase was used, the reactions it elicited, and how it affected relationships among staff members. As many participants as possible should join the discussion, citing similar or dissimilar experiences, and exploring ways that language can be interpreted differently in different situations and why this is.

➔ Again in groups of three, participants turn to The Language of Leadership (Figure 6.2). Each group has a copy, which it fills in with examples of leadership language, used or heard, that contribute to or detract from the development of shared leadership in their school. Groups should choose words and phrases bandied about in the halls or staff room that seem to have significant influence—or, on the other hand, very little influence—on major directions the school pursues or major decisions made in such areas as curriculum and assessment. In this quest, participants should not overlook language that is not necessarily meant to be negative but that discourages teachers from taking leadership. This can be language that they have heard others use or that they themselves have used. The Teachers as Leaders Framework, mounted on the wall, can stimulate participants to identify words and expressions used regularly in the school that either foster or detract from the fulfilment of the six characteristics of teacher leaders outlined in the framework.

➔ The task continues over the next 2 weeks, as participants at school listen carefully to discussions that reflect professional relationships, as played out in various locales and situations—staff room, playground, assembly, parent meetings, staff meetings, and collegial conversations. They try to identify phrases, terms, and expressions that demonstrate a broader view of leadership that includes idea generation, identification of key tasks, initiative taking, mutual influence, and shared responsibility. They also see if they can identify phrases, terms, and expressions that demonstrate a narrower definition that focuses on formal authority, the power of office, or the prerogatives of title. As they encounter these forms of language, they add them to their Language as Leadership Lists.

Figure 6.2. The Language of Leadership

Language Perceived as Supportive of Teacher Leadership and Parallel Leadership	Language Perceived as Detracting From Teacher Leadership and Parallel Leadership

➡ A week or more later, they hold a follow-up session. With the completed grid displayed on an overhead projector, participants react to the expanded inventory and discuss its implications. The purpose is to shape a rough consensus on the state of leadership language in the school. Through this, the group begins to understand the size and dimensions of their challenges—or, conversely, the extent of their support base—as teachers consider taking leadership in the school and as administrators consider the most useful forms of support to offer. Is the environment a favorable one, that is, is parallel leadership either an emerging reality or, at least, a real possibility in this school, or is the institution of teacher leadership going to be an uphill battle all the way? It is important for the group to have an accurate gauge of this crucial aspect of the school's culture before undertaking serious initiatives.

➡ With help of the facilitator, participants discuss the meaning and effect of certain phrases and words—and how they feel about that language. It is vital that participants speak openly and that terms are not regarded as negative if people in that school don't perceive them to be. Participants will benefit from listening to and exploring each other's views and values, and taking special notice of the positive language they want to see used in their school.

Exercises for Building a Base for Schoolwide Leadership

Exercise 6: Spots

Purpose. This exercise offers potential teacher leaders and the administrators who work with them an opportunity to explore the range of beliefs about teaching that exists in the school, and the dynamics involved in creating a schoolwide approach to teaching.

Rationale. The creation of a shared approach to teaching is one of the most important functions of school-based leadership. It cannot be achieved without building a professional learning community in which teacher leadership and parallel leadership are nurtured. In this exercise, participants reflect on their own beliefs about teaching and gain appreciation of their colleagues' beliefs. The exercise enables participants to experience directly what it means to be part of a professional learning community where staff members reflect together on common challenges, honor the multiplicity of perspectives among them, and work toward molding these perspectives into schoolwide processes that benefit students.

It is a simple truth that we are all captives of our own perspectives, our own ways of viewing the world. We fall prey easily to the misconception that other people think the same way we do about important matters. Of course, this is not true, and divisiveness within groups often results from this prevalent misconception. For a group to work effectively, individual members have to invest in understanding the viewpoints of their colleagues. This is especially true when the issues at hand are as complex and personal as those involved with teaching and learning—the focal points of teacher leadership.

This exercise beckons participants to understand that all members of a staff, although confronted with similar challenges, have different needs and inclinations. In the metaphor of the exercise, they all come from different spots. If they are to work together collaboratively, each staff member must understand something about what motivates other members. They must honor the spots others cherish almost as much as their own. In so doing, they can more easily find common ground on core challenges and use it to fulfill common cause.

Time Considerations and Necessary Materials. About 1 to 1½ hours are required for this exercise. Necessary materials include a "spot" for each participant, such as a piece of carpet or cardboard 1 foot (30 cm) square; participants' journals; a wall chart, poster, or transparency that succinctly recaps a significant teaching and learning challenge currently facing the school, for instance, better literacy practices or developing mutually respectful relationships among staff members and students outside the classroom; and a flipchart and markers.

Process

Important Note. The first part of this exercise involves individual reflective thought, a capacity that will support the leadership work that participants undertake together. The topic for reflection should be a major challenge facing the school in terms of teaching and learning. It should be an issue ripe for individual thought and group interaction, and one of significance to all participants. It should be expressed in a clear, concise sentence or two. Literacy, math skills, the role of the arts, higher-order thinking skills—these, along with others, some more specific—are examples of solid topics.

→ Participants confirm for each other, and with the facilitator, that they understand the topic for reflection. With that, each participant takes a spot, that is, a carpet or cardboard square. (The spot is meant to represent an individual's beliefs about the type of teaching most suited to the challenge as stated.) With spots in hand, participants go to a place within a defined area (their meeting room, an area beyond their meeting room, or, best of all, a green space near the school). They put down their square spots on the floor or ground and get comfortable on them. Participants should be far enough apart to be quietly alone, unable to converse with each other. Standing or sitting on their spots, they spend 15 minutes in silent solitude, reflecting on the challenge presented. They record their thoughts in their journals.

→ After about 15 to 20 minutes, participants reconvene in a central location—leaving their spot and journal behind at the place where they reflected on the challenge. The facilitator assists with the logistics. When gathered together, the group stands or sits in a circle for a short discussion that focuses on the following questions:

- What was it like to have your own place—your own spot?

- How did you react to being left alone for 15 minutes to think without interruption? What difference would it make if you regularly awarded yourself at work a short reflection time like the one you just had?

- Did any interesting revelations about yourself and your beliefs about teaching crop up while you were on your spot?

- What do your reflections say about your professional beliefs?

Important Note. A second part to this activity follows directly after the short discussion just held.

➡ With all participants maintaining physical contact with one another, they move to each person's spot in turn. They may discuss how this is to be done, but once the physically linked group is on the move, there is no more talking except at each spot. The group stops briefly at each spot, and the person whose spot it is may share, if he or she chooses, an insight that occurred at the spot about the selected challenge. This will be the only exception to the no-talk rule. Participants may also carry their journals and refer to them at their own spots.

➡ On the completion of the group's journey to all the spots, they return to the place where they started, for a fuller discussion. Questions include

- What strategy did the group adopt for getting itself around to everyone's spot? How was agreement on strategy reached?

- Who took the lead in this exercise? Why did you follow? Would you have followed the same person in another activity?

- How do you interpret the essential task of getting everyone around to every spot? What parallel does it have for your working together in the school? For leadership dynamics within the school?

- Referring to the discussion in Chapter 3 on professional learning communities, what parallels do you see between the concept of a professional learning community and getting the group to everyone's spot?

- How important is it to visit the spot of everyone you are working with on a common task? How important is this understanding when the work of the group is designing and carrying out learning experiences?

- What feelings did you experience during the exercise? How do these parallel your feelings about sharing perspectives on teaching practices?

- How did the written challenge look to you from other people's spots? What did you learn about others' needs, inclinations, or perspectives—both personally and professionally? How was the view from others' spots?

- What can you say about the extent to which members of this group honor each others' perspectives?

- What things can you do in your real work lives to ensure opportunity for reflection time by individuals and the group?

➜ Participants turn their attention to the responses they made to the challenge during their reflection time. They consult their journals and provide information for a group compilation of responses to the challenge—which a group member records on a poster-sized sheet of paper or flipchart.

➜ Finally, participants address this question, "If this is the sum total of what we can offer from our spots on this challenge, what are we equipped to do now?" In addressing this question, participants should recall the findings of research on effective practices—that is, that school improvement and reform are most effective and easily achieved when a whole-school approach to teaching is agreed on and undertaken.

➜ The discussion closes with participants reflecting aloud on the implications of this research for them in their journey towards school improvement.

Exercise 7: The Past

Purpose. Participants reflect on past interactions that have inhibited the growth of their professional community, and they seek to transcend these to establish mutual trust and a positive environment, one in which leadership can flourish.

Rationale. Leadership is about assuming responsibility for the future. Yet the past affects what people are able to do in the future. To move into the future with vigor and self-confidence, aspiring leaders have to position themselves in relation to the past that they share. If they do not do this consciously, then they risk paralysis at critical moments when what they need most is agility and flexibility. This exercise challenges participants to think critically about their shared past and to decide what posture to take with regard to prior events and interactions, especially ones that may be perceived as less than positive. The facilitator will find it useful, in guiding the dialogue, to be familiar, with the elements of emotional intelligence discussed by Goleman (1998).

A presumption underlying this exercise is that fixation with past events can inhibit effective group action in the future. Group members may rarely refer openly to the past, in the course of their work, but its events frequently lurk in the background, insert themselves into group deliberations, and affect the ability of a group to get its work done. If teacher leadership and parallel leadership are to be nurtured, mutual respect and trust must be present. An ethic of no blame has to exist, and the residue of past interactions has to be left behind.

In this exercise, it is highly unlikely that any of the details of participants' past interactions will be disclosed. Yet by publicly acknowledging that problematic interactions or events exist—without necessarily surfacing them or attempting to salve them—group members can unburden themselves. In coming to a common understanding of what to do about the past, they are able to deal more effectively with each other in the future. In the wake of the exercise, participants normally feel they are carrying less weight and are able to chart a freer course than they would have been otherwise.

Time Considerations and Necessary Materials. Normally, an hour will suffice for this exercise. Participants will need Post-it notes or small index cards large enough to write a sentence or two on, and a small cardboard container about the size of a cigar box.

Process

➡ Participants take two notes or cards, and write on each a brief description of a personal experience. One refers to a positive experience, a high, a memorable moment from their past work in this school. The second refers to a negative experience, one that sticks in their craw when they think about working in this school, one that they have not been able to get over or let go of, one they ponder when they are most down about what it means to work in this school. It helps when facilitators openly refer to their own experience to encourage participants to feel freer to write down theirs.

➡ After participants have done this, the facilitator collects the notes (not looking at them and not letting anyone else look at them) and places them in the cardboard box.

→ A discussion then ensues about what should be done with the box (and its contents, of course, both the positive notes and the negative ones). After the first volley or two of "toss it," "burn it," or "just read the positive ones," the group should settle into a more deliberative mode, focusing on what to do with the material in the box. Should anyone read the notes—the positive ones, or the negative ones, or both? If so, what should the person or persons do with this data? Summarize it for the group? For the head of the school? Perhaps the facilitator, in consultation with selected members of the group, should suggest who should read the notes and what form a report to the group should take? Ultimately, what should be done with the box of notes after the group deals with what is written on them? Trash it? Seal it and keep it in a safe place, but never open it?

→ Participants readily conclude that the questions about what to do and who should do it are sensitive and require thoughtfulness and a balancing of interests and perspectives. Matters of privacy weigh against the benefits of knowledge. A desire to put the past behind competes with understanding that the past will affect the future, no matter what. The facilitator encourages the group to wrestle with the difficult questions here and to reach conclusions that are fair and respectful to the individuals who comprise the group, yet useful and helpful to the group in fulfilling its collective aims.

→ After determining what to do with the contents of the box and the box itself, the group conducts a wrap-up discussion that focuses on the following questions:

- Going back over the ground you just covered in the discussion about how to handle positive and negative aspects of past working relationships in your school, describe the path you took as a group to reach your decisions.

- What would you say represented your most effective approach as a group to analyzing the problem?

- What explicit values are expressed by the group's decision about disposition of the contents of the box and the box itself? Are these values conducive to affirmative action?

- What does your group propose as three principles for moving on from a constraining past to a more positive future?

- What are the implications of your learning in this exercise for the leadership initiatives you are contemplating? Is the group equipped to take on some emotionally challenging work, or is it tentative?

The facilitator indicates that today's culminating reflection will focus on each individual's willingness to place past conflicts in perspective. Participants should examine their own attitudes and feelings about hanging on to old baggage, and assess how they might let go of that baggage to grow as individuals within the organization. Participants should refer to the three values underpinning successful parallel leadership found in Chapter 3 (mutual trust, individual expression, and shared purpose) and then ask themselves how this exercise illustrates each of the three values.

Exercise 8: Barriers

Purpose. Participants identify and come to terms with factors and forces that might prevent teacher leadership from flourishing in the school. In addition, participants are encouraged to explore how they might remove or circumvent these barriers in their quest for school revitalization and personal growth.

Rationale. Normally, the identification of constraints would follow the development of vision, strategy, and a tentative commitment to a set of initiatives. In this case, we believe there is good reason to make an initial scan of the obstructions to progress. Having completed the previous exercises, a group should be familiar with its major assets and liabilities. It should be aware of members' core values and beliefs and even have begun to envision initiatives that the group, or selected members, working together or individually, could undertake.

With this grounding and self-confidence, the group can afford to stand back and assess barriers, both external and self-imposed. Now they can tackle important challenges and gain ground toward their goals.

Time Considerations and Necessary Materials. This exercise normally takes 1 to 1½ hours. Have on hand a flipchart and markers and the Leadership Language grid produced in Exercise 5.

Process

➜ Participants begin by reviewing together the premises of teacher leadership discussed in Chapter 2. Initial discussion focuses on the following questions:

- Is there agreement that teacher leadership is real? What, then, are the implications for us personally and for the school?

- How is teacher leadership different from other forms of leadership, and do those differences show up in this school?

- Teacher leadership develops differently in different contexts, so what form might it take in this school?

➜ Having explored the premises and their bearing on the school, participants may have identified some barriers. In groups of three, they now brainstorm about barriers that stand in the way of making teacher leadership come alive in their school. Participants look at this issue from every angle (i.e., from the perspectives of teachers, principal, district and state administrators, parents, students). Groups record their responses on pages torn from a flipchart so they can be displayed later to the entire group.

➜ Participants discuss the following questions:

- Do the identified barriers fall into categories? (Different colored markers might be used for separate categories.)

- Which barriers do teachers put in their own way?

- Which are beyond teachers' control?

- Which can be circumvented or ignored?

➜ As the discussion progresses, participants move from identifying barriers and characterizing them to focusing on barriers that might budge if teachers, with the principal's support, worked at removing them. The touchstones for this part of the exercise are these questions:

- Which barriers might yield to establishing a firmer shared vision for school operations?

- Which might yield to more adept strategizing?

- Which, along these lines, might give way to political action by coalitions of teachers?

- Which might be alleviated through joint action with parents and community leaders?

Taking each malleable barrier in turn, participants generate additional flipchart pages full of ideas on how it might be overcome.

→ After discussing barriers and creating several pages of ideas on how to address a particular barrier, participants decide on specific steps that they can take to begin the process of overcoming barriers believed to be significantly inhibiting the development of teacher leadership in the school. They also note collective actions to take before their next session. Finally, participants record in their journals a specific action they will take as an individual to remove, overcome, or otherwise make obsolete, a barrier.

Exercise 9: Assumptions

Purpose. Participants examine their developmental work to date against a framework of important assumptions about teacher leadership.

Rationale. Theorists, including Argyris (1993), Schein (1992), Schon (1983), and Senge (1992), argue that people seeking to achieve organizational change need to uncover and examine the assumptions that guide their work. Only by examining these assumptions on a continuing basis can individuals and the group effectively assess their actions and align them with changing goals and circumstances.

The analysis that participants do in this exercise helps build the school's organizational learning capacity, which is exactly what is needed if they are to improve teaching and learning schoolwide. In effect, **teachers** who become adept at the sort of analysis that this exercise calls for are taking the lead in forming a professional learning community within their school.

By working through the exercise, participants acquire an analytic tool that can be used to support their work in both the short and long term. The framework that develops serves as a snapshot of the controlling assumptions that will guide the leadership initiatives participants are about to undertake. It serves also as a barometer for calibrating shifts in assumptions as those initiatives unfold.

Time Considerations and Necessary Materials. The exercise can normally be completed in an hour. Necessary materials include a flipchart

Table 6.2 A Framework of Assumptions

Schools do not need ⟷ leadership from teachers.	Schools need teacher leadership.
Teacher leadership is ⟷ distinctive.	Teacher leadership is like other forms of leadership.
Teaching and learning are ⟷ the focus of teacher leadership	Organizational issues are the focus of teacher leadership.
Teacher leaders are ⟷ identifiable in advance.	Teacher leaders may emerge unexpectedly.
Teacher leadership is ⟷ enduring and sustainable.	Teacher leadership is episodic and situational.
All teachers are potential ⟷ leaders.	Some teachers are potential leaders.
Teacher leadership can be ⟷ nurtured.	Teacher leadership is inherent.
Teachers are accountable ⟷ for learning outcomes.	Administrators are accountable for learning outcomes.
Teacher leaders work as ⟷ individuals.	Teacher leaders work in groups.
Teacher leaders are popular ⟷ with colleagues.	Teacher leaders are seen as difficult by colleagues.

and markers, an overhead projector with blank transparencies that can be written on, and the Framework of Assumptions (Table 6.2).

Process

→ Participants reflect on their current situation as encapsulated in the yield from previous exercises, including Readiness, The Power of Language, and Spots. They discuss what they have learned about their situation, together agree on some rough characterizations of it, and post these as bullet points on flipchart sheets.

→ Having posted on the wall the Framework of Assumptions, they continue their discussion, comparing their characterizations at the beginning of leadership development training with their current views of teacher leadership, using the assumptions in this framework as a guide. Note that the contrasting elements in the framework are extreme, with reality lying, in all likelihood, somewhere between the two positions. The following questions help center this discussion:

- What assumptions are reflected in our current circumstances?

- Where along the lines between the contrasting elements does our present situation best fit?

- Are there assumptions that influence our present situation that are not shown in the framework?

➜ When the group is decided on where, along each of the horizontal lines joining the sets of contrasting elements, their present situation falls, one member of the group records these on flipchart sheets or on a transparency.

➜ A discussion follows about assumptions and the effect they have on the way people work together and how assumptions might facilitate or impede progress as the group moves forward with its development. It is important here for participants to remind themselves of the unconscious nature of assumptions—often we are not aware of powerful assumptions that guide our actions, and we frequently have difficulty making our assumptions explicit.

➜ In closing, participants record in their journals a personal assumption about leadership in their school and the impact they believe it may have on the development of teacher leadership initiatives. Notes from this meeting, including frameworks participants wrote on, are kept for examination as the group continues its work, identifies and refines initiatives, and begins to implement them. Periodically, the group should revisit this material and refine it in light of new data emerging from the group's leadership initiatives.

Exercises for Actualizing Teacher Leadership for Successful School Revitalization

Exercise 10: Parallel Scenarios

Purpose. This exercise increases participants' understanding of the various forms parallel leadership can take in their school.

Rationale. Teacher leadership is a particular form of school leadership different from, yet highly dependent on, administrator support. For it to exist at all, moderate encouragement and support from administrators is required. For it to thrive, substantial encouragement and support are necessary. Thus teachers contemplating leadership initiatives should understand the nature and extent of parallel leadership as it exists in their school and the potential for its development. This exercise provides the opportunity to develop that understanding. Specifically, it invites participants to depict their organizational dynamics by grappling with a set of hypothetical scenarios for dealing with an educational challenge the school might well face. The assumption underlying it is that participants will, following the exercise, be able to imagine a richer set of possible leadership scenarios to fit the particular needs and conditions of their school.

Time Considerations and Necessary Materials. This exercise requires an hour or more to complete. Participants should have on hand: the definition of parallel leadership with its three defining characteristics (Chapter 3); the challenges for principals (Figure 3.1; Table 4.1) mounted on posters or wall charts; the snapshot from Chapter 3; the completed grid on leadership language (Exercise 5); an overhead projector and transparencies that can be written on; and a flipchart and markers.

Process

→ Participants begin by discussing the dynamics between administrator leaders and teacher leaders as described in the snapshot in Chapter 3. In the process, they review together the concept of parallel leadership and its accompanying characteristics, as outlined in Chapter 3, and the new roles of principals as outlined in Chapter 4.

→ Participants then read and briefly discuss the hypothetical, yet credible, challenge described below. They also read the four scenarios that follow the presentation of the problem.

The Problem. Chronic environmental problems—persistent automobile and residential fuel shortages, coupled with a series of floods caused by repeated clear-cutting near a bordering river—have finally captured the attention of community leaders in a small city. These leaders are now calling for businesses and social institutions, including schools, to do what they can to support more aggressive conservation measures. Schools, in particular, are asked to develop new approaches to the curriculum and to teaching that will increase students' understanding of ecological relationships and make them more knowledgeable about how communities can address proliferating, protracted environmental problems. A strong emphasis on total staff involvement—with planning efforts aimed at engaging students with real-world problems as part of their coursework—is essential.

The Scenarios

Scenario A. One member of the teaching staff is not only a creative thinker in fields related to the problem but also an instigator of change. She is fully prepared to recommend ways to address the problem. She begins to plan and initiate action. The principal supports, encourages, asks probing questions, talks up her initiative, and celebrates small successes as they occur—after he becomes convinced of the merits of the teacher's approach and sees the positive reactions of her colleagues. He has no perception of his authority being challenged but is a conservative thinker and so needs convincing when new ideas come into play.

Scenario B. A number of teachers, individually and in small groups, initiate and operate specific projects to address the problem in the context of the school's shared vision. They act independently and exhibit a high level of ownership for their initiatives and for the progress of students in the coursework that is developed. The principal, for her part, is perceived as a strong, somewhat larger-than-life leader. She generates enthusiasm for and through the common vision, and she encourages teachers as they look for ways to address the challenges in front of them. Teachers are supported, encouraged, and lauded by both the principal and their colleagues. The high level of energy in the school adds momentum to the teachers' efforts.

Scenario C. A small group of teachers advocate for and design change here. They understand the problem and are prepared to pose solutions. The principal, although working hard on behalf of the students, is fearful that these teachers somehow threaten the stability of the school and its community. Only when the principal sees that the teachers' initiatives can have a positive impact on the school, and that these successes will enhance his position as principal, does he become supportive and encouraging. There are frequent points of conflict between the teacher leaders and the principal.

Scenario D. The principal here has worked hard in the recent past at demonstrating instructional leadership in the school. She has a number of clear preconceptions about how the current challenge confronting the school should be addressed. Teachers, for their part, have normally receded in the face of initiatives advanced by the principal. Yet implementation of these initiatives has been episodic and uneven. The principal decides it is time to shift the balance of professional relationships, and she openly commits to the possibility that greater leadership by teachers at this juncture might produce more positive schoolwide effects.

➔ Participants break into four work groups. Each group is assigned one of the four scenarios. In their discussions, each group describes, as specifically as possible, what might occur in the situation as posed. After the group has catalogued events they imagine would occur in the hypothetical school, they outline a possible response to the situation if it were to occur in their own school. The following questions can assist with both assignments:

- What do you envision the teacher or teachers doing?

- What do you envision the principal doing?

- What kind of initiatives might each take?

- What obstacles might the teacher or teachers have to overcome?

- How would authority be apportioned between teachers and administrators?

- How might responsibilities be allocated, relationships managed, and tasks carried out?

- Who would be held responsible for outcomes?

- What ramifications would all this have on the leadership dynamics in the school?

➔ The whole group reconvenes to talk in depth about the following sorts of issues, in light of their small-group discussions:

- What impact does the relationship between principal and teachers have on the success of school initiatives?

- What difference does it make if the principal initiates an action or if a teacher or teachers initiate it?

- Contrast the dynamics, as you imagine them, between the four scenarios, were they at work in your school.

- And a question of paramount importance: What impact could the initiation of parallel leadership have on student outcomes in your school?

➜ Finally, the participants, as a whole group, bring their attention back to the three values of parallel leadership and pose this question for individual reflection: What can I do to foster one of these values in our school? After a short reflection time, participants record their intended action in their journals, in the form of a specific action that they might take in light of a challenge like the one posed in this exercise.

Exercise 11: Imagine!

Purpose. This exercise extends emerging leadership concepts into images that may be used to guide emerging teacher leadership initiatives.

Rationale. The aim is for participants to gain a deeper, broader understanding of the kind of leadership that can undergird the initiatives they will design and implement in the months and years ahead. The means for achieving this goal is the creation of visual images for the kind of leadership participants would like to see develop in their school.

Your visual images may be figures like most of the ones on the wall or a metaphor. *Metaphor* is defined later in this exercise on page 120. The principal advantage of a visual image is that it provides an opportunity for people to be expansive in their thinking without having to confront directly and in detail all the consequences. Visual images engender creativity and inspire a freedom of spirit on the part of participants, urging them to shake their daily routine, reach for boldness, and imagine a wide-ranging set of possibilities. Perhaps most important, visual image making can build commitment to a shared view of a desired future.

Time Considerations and Necessary Materials. The first and third segments of the exercise can be accomplished in about an hour. Included in the first is an initial consideration—and generation—of visual images by small groups. Included in the third is deliberation by the whole group, leading to consensus on the visual images. Between the first and third segments, the small groups meet to refine their thinking. This might consume an additional hour. Needed for the exercise are an overhead projector and transparencies that can be written on; a flipchart and markers; and Figures 6.3 through 6.7, which are visual images that relate to educational leadership. Copies of these should be posted on the wall.

Figure 6.3

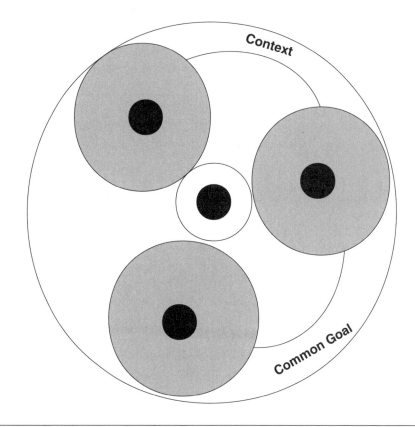

Process

→ Participants gather and discuss the main task of this exercise—to develop visual images that represent the approach to leadership the group believes to be most suited to its workplace. These images will serve as a continuing source of guidance as the group proceeds. The visual images may also reflect the different examples of parallelism described in Chapter 3, that is, parallelism viewed musically, artistically, literarily, philosophically, technologically, and mathematically. Participants might comment on how they relate personally to each example.

→ Participants form concentric circles—one circle standing inside another circle. Each circle should contain four to six people; the two circles together contain no more than 12 people, or six in each circle. Each circle must contain the same number of people—four, five, or six.

Figure 6.4

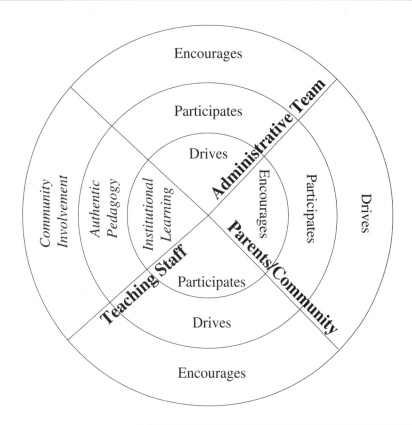

More than one set of circles can be set up, depending on the size of the group. Those in the inner of the two circles face outward, and those in the outer circle face inward, so every participant is facing one other person.

→ Participants collectively choose one figure posted on the wall to concentrate on, and in pairs discuss (a) the aspects, attributes, and dimensions that the figure produces in their minds and (b) how appropriate the image is to the sort of leadership dynamic they are attempting to create in the school. Because there will be only a short time—less than 5 minutes—for conversation in each of the pairs, participants should be prepared to share air time equally with their partners. After about 5 minutes, at a signal from the facilitator, participants cease conversation, and those in the outer circle move one person to the right.

Figure 6.5

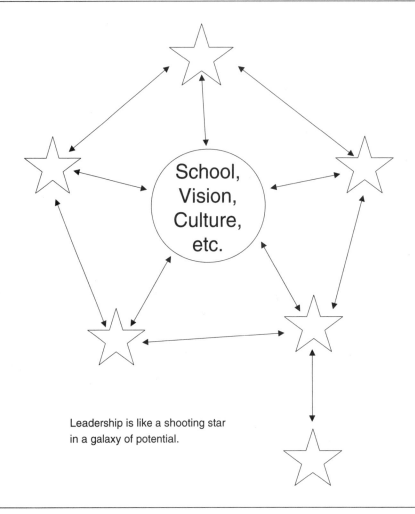

School,
Vision,
Culture,
etc.

Leadership is like a shooting star
in a galaxy of potential.

➡ Participants turn their attention to another of the figures on the wall and address the same issues they did with the first. After about 5 minutes, conversation ceases, and those in the outer circle again shift one person to the right. This process of shifting and conversing with a new partner is repeated for the fourth and fifth figures.

➡ Participants then dissolve their concentric circles and come together to discuss their principal task, which is to generate a visual image of their own. It may also be useful for group members to cite some of

Figure 6.6

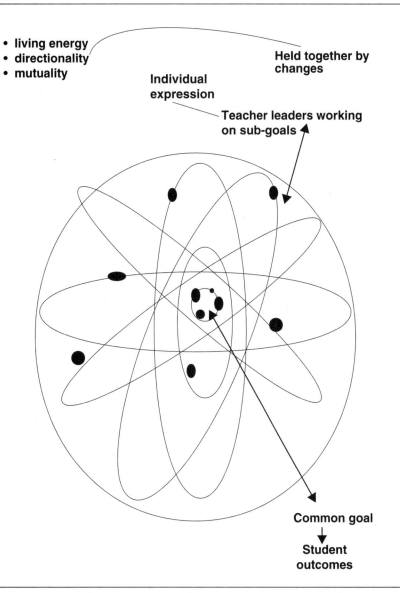

- **living energy**
- **directionality**
- **mutuality**

Held together by changes

Individual expression

Teacher leaders working on sub-goals

Common goal

Student outcomes

the observations that were exchanged in the concentric-circle conversations, on the assumption that this exchange will help the group devise its own visual images. The following description of the task may usefully be displayed as a transparency.

Figure 6.7

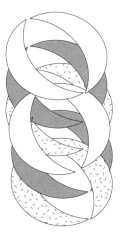

Create a visual image for leadership as you would like to see it develop in your school. The image may be a diagram (like several of the figures on the wall) or a metaphor. A *metaphor* is a word, object, action, or concept used to represent a different word, object, action, or concept—as a means to illuminate understanding. For example, "A teacher leader is a lighthouse in stormy seas" is a metaphor. A metaphorical visual image might show a teacher leader standing, larger than life, on a rock in stormy seas, with rays of light radiating from her or his head. Think pictures first. Add words later, if necessary, and stick to only a few. Remember that you are trying to capture the essence of both the teacher leadership initiatives you intend to undertake and the relationship you intend to forge with the administrative leadership in the school.

➔ The whole group breaks into small groups of three each, to generate their own visual images of leadership. When they have accomplished this, the day's session ends. However, the exercise carries over into the next several days, offering the small groups enough time to refine their visual images and prepare them for display in the group's meeting room.

➔ At the group's next work session, participants view the refined images developed by the small groups and discuss the educational values underlying each. Visual images that lack educational justification should either be eliminated or reformulated. Participants then decide which of the images (could be more than one) will represent the approach to leadership that group members propose to take. Based on these discussions, self-selected group members agree to refine the chosen pictorial representations as necessary so that they can be presented at the group's next work session. The chosen images remain on display in the group's meeting room as the group plans, implements, and evaluates its actions in the months ahead.

Exercise 12: Lights! Action!

Purpose. Participants translate leadership capacity built in previous exercises into a set of initiatives responsive to the school's declared vision.

Rationale. Nearly every school has a vision statement. Usually, it is prominently displayed in a public place in the school. Through this exercise, participants assess whether and how what happens in the classroom matches the school's vision. With this analysis in hand, teachers, with administrators' support, shape initiatives that they believe will better fulfill their declared aspirations, in keeping with a schoolwide approach to teaching, learning, and assessment.

Whether the alignment of actions with vision promotes long-term school improvement is debatable. Some would argue that most school vision statements are uninspiring, and virtually no one in the school takes them seriously. We believe that the effort and energy that go into creating these statements of intent ought to be honored and that consistency between aspirations and actions is integral to forward movement. At the very least, the statements provide a useful platform for assessing actions that teachers consider worthy.

As aspiring leaders, participants have shared a range of experiences since Group Portrait and Oops! They have explored colleagues' values, beliefs, and qualities, and have become aware of the effects of their language and underlying assumptions on their actions. They have considered the leadership concepts presented in Part 1. They are aware of the effects of the way staff members talk to each other and of the assumptions that drive action in the school. They are aware of the range and diversity of members' values and beliefs about teaching and learning. They are sober about major barriers in the path of leadership initiatives they may undertake. And they can describe in graphic terms the kind of shared leadership they want to bring to the school. Equipped in these ways, participants should be prepared now to frame initiatives and shape activities that are consistent with the stated vision for the school. In addition, they should be prepared to assess the value of the stated vision and suggest changes that might better serve the changing needs of those whom the school serves.

Time Considerations and Necessary Materials. The exercise can take up to 2 hours. The school's vision statement should be displayed on a poster or wall chart in the group's meeting room. Also needed are a flipchart and markers, the Teachers as Leaders Framework (Table 1.1), and the Diagram Linking Parallel Leadership and Successful School Reform (Figure 3.1). A room with plenty of open floor space is required.

Process

➡ Participants stand in a circle. At the outset, the exercise involves much moving about, quick thinking, and careful listening. It will help if participants read the exercise description a few days ahead of doing it and formulate ideas on what they might contribute.

➡ Participants take turns stepping into the middle of the circle and making a statement about initiatives or actions they wish to take to support the vision of the school. The statements should be something a teacher wants to do that is a step in the direction of realizing the vision. *Doing* and *action* are the operative words here. All the statements should begin with the phrase, "All my colleagues who . . . , step into the circle." Other participants who can personally identify with the substance of the statement, in that it could involve them as well, should move into the center of the circle, take a moment to look at who else is there, and then step back. After one person starts the process, a second person steps into the center quickly and repeats the process. Examples might be, "All my colleagues who will reach out to the community for support of a student service project, step into the circle," or "All my colleagues who will devise special ways of supporting students with language difficulties, step into the circle." People step into the center and back into the circle rim as appropriate. Then others take their turns, making a statement of their own and testing its appeal to others.

➡ After 20 to 30 minutes of the circle, participants reassemble in an area where they can sit down. They recall as many of the actions as they can, and someone records them on a flipchart. The list should be as exhaustive as possible. The group then considers what the list says about participants' combined efforts, the work they are doing or planning, and the contributions and aspirations of the group as whole.

➜ At this point, participants pause and find the relevance of the actions they have cited to pertinent sections in the previous chapters. Direct references ought to be made to the Teachers as Leaders Framework (Table 1.1), the Diagram Linking Parallel Leadership and Successful School Reform (Figure 3.1), and snapshots that illustrate the fulfilment of school vision or the dynamics of improving teaching, learning, and assessment schoolwide.

➜ Participants again review the list of actions on the flipchart and discuss what the material says about their leadership, actual and potential, individual and collective. Summarizing statements could include assertions like these: "We can do important things together, some in subgroups, and some as individuals." "Our planned actions reflect more assertive forms of leadership than our present actions." "What we plan to do is remarkably consistent with the Teachers as Leaders Framework."

➜ As a concluding element, participants write in their journals one action they can take in the short term that will move the school toward fulfilling its vision. They should describe this action in concrete terms, being clear about what steps they will take to accomplish it.

Exercise 13: Staff Meeting

Purpose. The group uses a particular real-world challenge to assess its own progress in terms of what it has learned about teacher leadership and parallel leadership.

Rationale. The group could perform any number of tests to see if it is ready to take on leadership for school reform. This exercise is especially apropos because it focuses on an event that exists in one form or another in almost all schools. Staff meeting time is precious because it is a rare opportunity for deliberative action. It is, in many schools, the only time that all staff members gather to address issues of common concern. Thus it provides a challenging venue where participants can test some of the ideas developed in previous exercises. Teachers generally tend to be frustrated by the way staff meetings unfold, cynical about their usefulness under most circumstances, and generally unclear about steps that might be taken to improve them—or at least make them tolerable. In all too many schools, staff meetings are little more than platforms for information sharing or for wrestling with current problems.

Time Considerations and Necessary Materials. The exercise should take 1 to 2 hours. Participants should have on hand an overhead projector and transparencies to write on; a flipchart and markers; work products from previous exercises, such as the group's envisioned initiatives from Exercise 12, the visual image or images from Exercise 11, the outline of assumptions from Exercise 9, and the language grid from Exercise 5.

Process

➔ Participants briefly review what they have accomplished in terms of developing their leadership capacity. Within this context, they discuss a new task: designing a structure and agenda for a staff meeting grounded in the group's interpretation of teacher leadership and parallel leadership and its envisioned leadership actions. The proposed structure and agenda would advance the leadership work teachers are about to undertake. That this work should be done in partnership with the principal is a given. But *partnership* is the operant word. Here is the task:

> Design a structure and format for your school's next staff meeting. Identify key issues that should be addressed in the meeting, and outline procedures for addressing them. Ground your proposal in concepts of teacher leadership and parallel leadership. Consider the following:
>
> - Goals and outcomes sought
>
> - Necessary agenda items
>
> - Sequence of items—important first, trivial last
>
> - Need for, and role of, chair or facilitator
>
> - Necessary prior preparation for the meeting
>
> - Guidelines for discussion, deliberation, and decision making
>
> - Professional development and growth potential that can be built into the meeting
>
> Ensure that your proposal engages participants in the meeting and produces "mileage and momentum" rather than "pablum and paralysis."

➜ Work on the task begins in small groups of three participants each. They discuss possible structures for the meetings in general and also generate specific agenda items that are consequential.

➜ Following these small-group interactions, time is allocated for all to share, discuss, and critique each other's ideas. At this point, participants might turn to the frameworks discussed earlier to discern whether their proposals are consistent with the spirit of teacher leadership and parallel leadership: Teachers as Leaders Framework (Table 1.1), Diagram Linking Parallel Leadership and Successful School Reform (Figure 3.1), and the Framework of Assumptions (Table 6.2).

➜ The whole group, using discussion skills perfected in previous exercises, formulates a single compelling proposal for staff meetings, including format, agendas for the next several meetings, and shared facilitation responsibilities.

➜ The final question the group should address is what to do with its proposal now. Participants should assume clear responsibility for the next steps—identifying specific actions that are consistent with the principles of shared leadership as they have developed.

Exercise 14: Six Months Later and Beyond

Purpose. The exercise draws participants into a process of tracing and documenting ways in which teacher leadership and parallel leadership have impacted their school.

Rationale. In undertaking this activity 6 months later, a year later, and a year and a half later, after working through the preceding 13 exercises, participants look critically at the effect their efforts as teacher leaders are having on the school, including students, staff, and community. Use here is made of a process of backward mapping (Padilla et al., 1996). Through this exercise, participants evaluate the authenticity and impact of their professional learning on a continuing basis, and they accrue insights into ways that leadership relates to school outcomes.

Time Considerations and Necessary Materials. This exercise requires a couple of hours each time it is done. Participants need their leadership development journals and the group's key instruments from its leadership development portfolio. In addition, the Diagram Linking Parallel Leadership and Successful School Reform (Figure 3.1) on a poster, a wall chart, or a transparency—is the principal focus for the backward mapping that participants do. The backward mapping questions in 3 and 6 below should also be on a transparency. Finally, a flipchart should be available.

Process

➡ Given that this exercises causes the group to reassemble after a period of time, it is important to begin by recounting highlights of the developmental journey that both the group and individuals have taken. Participants reflect openly on a moment, incident, activity, or discussion that was a significant growth point, either for them individually or for the group as a whole.

➡ The group then identifies something significant that has happened in the school as a result of their leadership development efforts, or something, in particular, that has contributed to improved outcomes. The group may need to discuss this for a time to identify and agree on particular events, shifts, or moments that were significant. Examples may relate to student outcomes, collaborative planning, collegial support, or effective community interchange.

➡ Participants consider the following four questions in relation to the occurrence referred to in the preceding paragraph. Each question is considered individually, with enough time to discuss their ideas about it.

- What was the nature and extent of educational improvement?

- What factors were perceived to be responsible for the improvement?

- What roles did individuals and groups play in bringing about the improvement?

- What leadership dynamics underpinned the improvement?

➡ As each question is considered, a member of the group summarizes the responses on a flipchart page.

➡ Participants then turn their attention to the Diagram Linking Parallel Leadership and Successful School Reform (Figure 3.1) and address this question: "Does what we have come up with in our responses to the questions support or refute the conclusion represented the diagram?"

➜ Discussion concludes with participants discussing the following questions:

- How might *enhanced school capacity* be defined?

- How have leadership dynamics in the school shifted over the past 6, 12, or 18 months?

- How sustainable are the new leadership dynamics?

- How can we use the understanding we have attained here to enhance school capacity further and thus continue to improve student outcomes?

Overview of the Teachers as Leaders Research Design

Background

The research that provided the basis for this book was conducted in three phases over a 5-year period. The first two phases were completed in Queensland, Australia, with the financial support of the Queensland Education Department and the Australian Research Council. The third phase was undertaken as part of an Australia-wide project, with links to Michigan. Phase three was funded by the Australian Commonwealth Department of Education, Training and Youth Affairs (DETYA) and the Australian Research Council.

Phase One: Year One (1996)

Research began in disadvantaged communities in the Wide Bay Region of Queensland. The initial purpose was to illuminate the work of extra-ordinary teachers whose effects on their schools and communities had won the acclaim of their principals and of their colleagues. Some had addressed complex issues involving rural isolation; others had achieved success amid serious prejudice and cultural conflict in Aboriginal communities; and still others had confronted the effects of high-level unemployment in communities where generations of unemployment had been the norm. The following questions guided Phase-One research:

1. What characteristics distinguish the work of classroom teachers who have achieved notable success and influence in working in socioeconomically disadvantaged schools?

2. What forms of leadership, if any, are inherent in those characteristics?

The following four criteria were created to identify suitable teachers for the research:

1. Concrete evidence of significant contributions to an aspect of social justice in their school or school community

2. High esteem in the community, particularly among socioeconomically disadvantaged individuals and groups

3. Colleagues' recognition of their influence on school decision making

4. A high level of school-based responsibility accorded by colleagues and the school administration

Fifteen school-based educators were identified through these criteria, and all agreed to participate in the project on the understanding that their involvement would afford them meaningful professional development. Two distinct outcomes emerged from this first phase: a preliminary teachers as leaders framework and a definition of teacher leadership.

The results of Phase One were published in Crowther and Olsen (1996) and Crowther (1996).

Phase Two: Years Two to Four (1997 to 1999)

The two stages of Phase Two were as follows:

1. Further exploration and validation of the preliminary teachers as leaders framework

2. Development of leadership materials and processes to implement the refined framework

The following three questions guided this phase of the research work:

1. What aspects of the preliminary teachers as leaders framework appear valid?
2. What changes to the preliminary framework appear necessary?
3. What are the key characteristics of a validated framework?

The research was conducted in six schools in disadvantaged communities in Queensland. School administrators, system officials, and teachers in socioeconomically disadvantaged schools were invited to identify highly successful educational responses to a school-initiated reform. Innovative practices that were explored included the following:

- Restructuring of a high school program to enhance student retention and vocational placements
- Successful establishment of an alternate-campus educational facility for street kids
- Development of a highly effective cultural-literacy program in a migrant center
- Implementation of a program that involved indigenous parents in student literacy development and community problem solving

The principal research processes used during the Phase-Two research were

- On-site analyses of the four case study situations, using observations, interviews, and interactional analysis techniques
- Focus groups involving participants from the schools and members of the research team
- Postresearch analysis and synthesis of the research outcomes by the research team, including validation of these outcomes by the project participants

Data analysis conducted during Phase Two confirmed the essential features of the preliminary teachers as leaders framework but also suggested two necessary adjustments. The first was clearer acknowledgement of the centrality to teacher leaders of teaching, learning, and assessment than the preliminary framework contained. This consideration is incorporated in the framework presented in Table 1.1. The second was that the full maturation of teacher leadership required the encouragement of principals and system administrators, and this aspect should be explored fully in the next phase of the research. Parallel leadership was identified as important at this stage but not defined or conceptualized. Critical analysis of Phase-One and Phase-Two outcomes was completed through an international on-line conference convened by the Australian Council for Educational Administration in September 1999.

Phase Three: Years Four and Five (1999-2000)

Phase Three built on Phase Two. The Innovation and Best Practice Project (IBPP) was instrumental here. A project of the Australian Commonwealth Department of Education, Training and Youth Affairs, IBPP was directed by Professor Peter Cuttance of the University of Sydney and involved a consortium of four Australian Universities: Sydney, Melbourne, Edith Cowan, and Southern Queensland. It was one of the largest educational research projects ever undertaken in Australia, involving 107 schools from all states and territories. Each school researched and reported on innovative practices designed to improve learning outcomes for students, with guidance provided by accredited external specialists—mainly, university researchers.

Nine of the 107 IBPP schools—identified as having enhanced student achievement in literacy or mathematics as a result of a school-based innovation—were selected for specialized analysis of their leadership dynamics by the University of Southern Queensland IBPP team. The nine schools were located in three Australian States (Queensland, New South Wales, Victoria) and encompassed public, Catholic, and independent systems as well as elementary and secondary levels.

Four questions provided the structure for the Phase-Three research:

1. What was the nature and extent of the measured improvement in student achievement?

2. What factors were perceived by teachers and administrators as accounting for this improvement?

3. What roles did individuals and groups play in bringing about the documented improvement in student achievement?

4. What leadership dynamics underpinned the improvement?

Researchers, working in pairs, employed a backward mapping strategy (Padilla, Trevino, Gonzalez, & Trevino, 1996) in Phase Three. Student achievement data in a key learning area (literacy or mathematics) were scrutinized for empirical validity. Brief summaries of the findings from two of the case study schools, relative to research questions 1, 2, and 3, are contained in Table A.1. Research question 4 was explored through focus groups involving members of the participating school teams.

As a result of Phase-Three research, the concept of parallel leadership was clarified and confirmed. The link between parallel leadership and school capacity building, as outlined in Chapter 3, was also explored. Additionally, conceptual links between parallel leadership and enhanced outcomes were established. These are captured in Chapter 4. External validation of Phase-Three outcomes was then undertaken through face-to-face discussion with a range of educational groups in Michigan. A summary of the Michigan findings is contained in Appendix B. Upon completion of Phase-Three research, further analysis was undertaken of the supportive efforts of four of the case study principals. Through individual interviews, we inquired into their roles in nurturing teacher leadership initiatives. The following four aspects of their work were explored:

1. The principals' conception of educational leadership

2. The distinction between principal leadership and teacher leadership

3. The strategies and activities used to encourage, nurture, and develop teacher leadership

4. The perceived outcomes of teacher leadership

From this inquiry, the research team formulated the seven challenges for the principal in nurturing teacher leadership. These are recounted in Chapter 4. The results of the Phase-Three research are published in Crowther, Hann, and McMaster (2001) and in Cuttance (2001).

Limitations

Our research to date has two important limitations. First, it was conducted in schools where successful reform seemed to be widely accepted as achievable. Therefore leadership concepts and processes that

Table A.1. Research Schools: A Summary of Outcomes and Factors Perceived as Important in Contributing to Successful Innovation in Two IBPP Schools

Elements	*West Town High School*
Outcomes	Improved basic math as well as applied-mathematics skills in year 8. Improved parent and student attitudes toward the school. Enhanced school image in the community.
Strategic Foundations	Initiated by mathematics department head to improve student achievement and nurture love of math. Principal supported on basis of consistency with school vision.
Cohesive Community	Strong alignment between principal, department head, and teacher/coordinator. Powerful parent and student support. Labor relations (industrial) issues caused some teachers concern.
Infrastructural Design	Movable partitions replaced fixed walls. School day extended. Supportive math curriculum developed for underachieving, disadvantaged students.
Schoolwide Teaching and Learning	Emphasis on real-life math applications. Specialist community resource persons brought into the school. Enhanced student engagement through small group activities. On-the-spot access to teacher consultations.
Professional Support	Large budget for professional development. Special program funding accessed. Principal and senior management supported the initiative.
Synthesis	This project was distinguished by the initiative of the department head, principal, and teacher in challenging labor relations (industrial) circumstances. Vision based in department head's and teacher's love of mathematics. Initiative implemented through radical modifications to time, space, and teaching strategies. Abandoned temporarily with changes in administration and time-tabling limitations.

continued

Table A.1. Continued

Elements	*Sunbeach High School*
Outcomes	Improved literacy skills, particularly in years 1 and 4 (tested at years 1, 4, 7). Improved student attitudes, particularly in year 4. Schoolwide adoption of the literacy program substantiated by year-4 success. Improved public image of education.
Strategic Foundations	Initiated by learning-support teacher inspired by eye-opening professional development experience. Strong principal and district director facilitation throughout. School vision modified in response to success of innovation.
Cohesive Community	Schoolwide workshops implemented by two teachers with principal's encourage-ment. Strong parent support and involvement.
Infrastructural Design	Staged trial used to implement and test effects. Flexible school mechanisms facilitated implementation.
Schoolwide Teaching and Learning	Focus on metacognitive approach to literacy. Explicit phoneme/grapheme instruction emphasized.
Professional Support	Teacher-initiated special funding. School-based funding of professional develop-ment. Links established with other schools for professional development.
Synthesis	Derived from energy and conviction of a teacher. Consistency with school vision, and support of principal, important factors. Program not so consistently success-ful in other local schools, pointing to importance of particularistic factors at Sunbeach.

emerged from the research might not have similar application in schools with a history of apathy or failed reform. Second, most of the Phase-Three case studies that were integral to the development of the concept of parallel leadership featured reforms that were not initiated as whole-school reform but, rather, were developed from smaller, classroom-based innovations. Therefore all the dynamics of whole-school reform might not have been taken into account in our conceptualization of leadership for successful school reform. In the interpretation of conclusions emanating from the research, these important limitations should be considered. Because of them, we regard our research as incomplete and are seeking ways to extend it.

Australian Case Study Schools

Phase One

Cherbourg State School, Cherbourg, Queensland

Imbil State School, Imbil, Queensland

Murgon State School, Murgon, Queensland

Goondiwindi State High School, Goondiwindi, Queensland

Nanango State School, Nanango, Queensland

Nanango State High School, Nanango, Queensland

Proston State School, Proston, Queensland

Tin Can Bay State School, Tin Can Bay, Queensland

Phase Two

Cairns Consortium of Schools, Manunda, Queensland

Goondiwindi State High School, Goondiwindi, Queensland

Kingaroy State School, Kingaroy, Queensland

Milpera State High School, Chelmer, Queensland

Stradbroke State School, Stradbroke Island, Queensland

Nanango State High School, Nanango, Queensland

Bendigo Senior Secondary College, Bendigo, Victoria

Christian Community High School, Regents Park, New South Wales

Emmaus Catholic College, Erskine Park, New South Wales

Glen Waverly Secondary College, Glen Waverly, Victoria

Harristown State High School, Toowoomba, Queensland

Mount Pritchard East Public School, Mt. Pritchard, New South Wales

Pomona State School, Pomona, Queensland

Stuartholme School, Toowong, Queensland

Westfields Sports High School, Fairfield West, New South Wales

A Report on the Michigan Review

With the new millennium just underway, the authors organized a series of focus groups and interviews in Michigan to subject the ideas in this book to the scrutiny of teachers, professors of teacher education and educational administration, and other higher education leaders. Four focus groups were held, one with faculty and graduate students at Michigan State University College of Education; a second with teachers and staff from the Michigan Education Association; a third with faculty and administrators from several institutions serving the educational needs of Northern Lower Michigan; and a final one with teachers at Novi, in Southeast Michigan, associated with the Galileo Project (the purpose of which is to create an ongoing forum for teacher leaders to discuss issues of common concern).

These focus groups and interviews pointed to the promise and the problems in the path of teacher leadership. We recount both here. First, the promise is depicted in an interview with the Michigan Teacher of the Year 2000, a person who immediately resonated with the ideas in this book, seeing herself as a teacher leader and perceiving the potential in many of her colleagues. Following the interview report is a rendering of a set of challenging issues that were raised in the several focus groups held in mid-2000.

The Promise: A Perspective on Teacher Leadership From a Teacher Leader

Margaret Holtschlag, Michigan Teacher of the Year 2000, and one of four finalists for the US Teacher of the Year award, is one of those thousands of classroom teachers about whom this book is written: not just an outstanding teacher, an innovative curriculum designer, and a mentor of professional colleagues, but also a true leader in her own right. Here, Margaret discussed with Steve Kaagan (in East Lansing, Michigan, May 2000) the concept of teacher leadership, the Teachers as Leaders Framework in particular, and its relevance to her work.

Kaagan: What do teachers who want to continue their classroom teaching do to lead? How does teacher leadership differ from administrator leadership?

Holtschlag: Teacher leadership starts with a teacher who gets an idea, an idea related to student learning or to making teaching more vibrant. Teacher leadership activities are essentially intrinsic, born of a need to bring all that we can to our children. With an idea in hand, be it about writing or something else, a teacher goes to another teacher or group of teachers and gets them excited about working on the idea. Then a core of people come together to do something significant.

School improvement teams (diverse groups mandated by state law to improve the school's performance) can be places where teacher leadership thrives. Yet these teams operate, for the most part, in a top-down way. Their work originates with the principal, who pulls together a group to work on schoolwide problems. In some, but not all, instances, the agenda of these teams is school improvement. But in almost all instances, the agenda matches what administrators had in mind in the first place. The origins were not teachers' views of what needs to be done to improve teaching and learning.

Kaagan: You have seen our tentative Framework for Teacher Leadership, with its six elements (publicly articulates a better view of the world, generates authenticity in teaching, fosters sincerity and trust, confronts structural barriers, builds networks of support, and nurtures a culture of success). Is the framework an accurate rendering of what teacher leadership is all about?

Holtschlag: I was talking with another state teacher of the year recently who was questioning her role and place as a teacher, and I referred to the framework as a means of offering her validation. I was saying, in effect, it's okay to be a teacher leader; go ahead and allow yourself; this is you. She was very grateful.

Any one of the elements in the framework is a fine quality. "Publicly articulates a better view of the world" conveys a really positive outlook. I am fortunate in my school, because the attitude among the staff is quite positive. However, one could focus in on a quality like "confronts structural barriers" and say that a teacher who exhibits this capacity is a troublemaker. I don't believe that to be so, but it is one element that some may perceive as two-edged.

Another way to respond to your question is to ask, what about a teacher who doesn't show one of the qualities, but shows the other five? For example, the teacher who "fosters sincerity and trust" but does not "generate authenticity in teaching." Under these circumstances, a teacher would be emitting positive affect but without a foundation in teaching behind it. In the absence of knowing what really works for effective teaching and learning, then all the fostering of sincerity and trust might be empty. On the other hand, if a teacher knows what makes something effective for our children, but does not have communication skills or social rapport, this, too, would be a serious shortfall. So, in the final analysis, I come to the conclusion that all six are essential.

When we discussed the framework at the Education Association meeting a few weeks ago, the focus was on the difficulty for many of overcoming structural barriers. From my point of view, the exercise involved with this element is to keep trying until one gets to *yes*. Yet I also believe that if administrators are not open to teacher initiative, teacher leadership will inevitably stay small. I worked in a district once where the principal said, "What you're doing is good, but couldn't you put the desks back into rows?" Another colleague and I were doing some really interesting things with our kids, but under these circumstances, couldn't take it very far. So I finally had to make a decision to move on to another school.

Kaagan: If teacher leadership were an accepted part of a school's functioning, how would the relationship between teachers and administrators shift?

Holtschlag: You have to understand that in many instances, teacher leadership involves a teacher's presenting an idea whose worth has not been proven yet. So, in all likelihood, the administrator does not see the reason for pursuing the idea. The basic shift in the relationship between teachers and administrators, where teacher leadership is present, is that administrators exhibit faith in the professionalism of the teachers to pursue their ideas. They trust that it's going to be okay.

Power plays are not part of this shift in relationship. I noted that power was not explicitly mentioned in the framework. Yes, there probably would be a power shift in the relationship between teachers and administrators if teachers were leading. But power shift has too much of a negative connotation. I prefer to say that there would be more of a shared responsibility and mutual honoring for each of the people involved, more like we are all working together, more of a partnership.

I recognize that this idea of shared responsibility does not fit the traditional administrative model. A parallel here is what has happened with the old notion that the teachers know all, and the children come to them as empty vessels. That's passed by the wayside. So, too, should the idea that the administrator knows all. Teachers, in fact, come to the table with ideas and decision-making skills of their own.

Kaagan: If teacher leadership were an accepted part of a school's functioning, how would the public respect afforded teachers be affected?

Holtschlag: Oh man, wouldn't that be cool? There would not only be a quite rapid increase in public respect for teachers and for the profession, there would be a lot more community participation in what's going on in the school. Take, for example, a teacher at my school who's doing something very positive with literacy. If she were nurtured in that work and given the space to do that work, there would be a ripple effect, and parents and community would be drawn in to build on the positive effects. After all, don't most people want to become involved with people who are putting into action good ideas? You want to learn from them and contribute to them. I believe that communities everywhere want to be a greater part of what's going on in schools. And this extends beyond the current drives for accountability. Teacher leadership, in effect, could be a powerful way of shaping and making real a shared vision for student learning in the school, between the school staff and the community.

Kaagan: If teacher leadership were an accepted part of a school's functioning, what would be the effect on student outcomes?

Holtschlag: Huge! With the situation of community members who do not have any buy-in to what is going on in the school, there is a lack of respect, and this lack of respect is transmitted to our children. Under these circumstances, the school is functioning in an isolated way. If, on the other hand, there is a push by the school to engage the community in the work of the school; if teachers take, and are encouraged to take, initiatives that do invite the community in, in integral ways, the children get the message that their learning is important, and they react accordingly.

Kaagan: Anything I should have asked and didn't?

Holtschlag: Just a couple of final observations. It's not easy to bring lots of people into the process. Teacher leadership takes tons of time—some of it wasted. And one makes a lot of mistakes along the way. I tend to go from one thing to another, to keep on adding things to bring to my teaching. For example, I paired with another teacher once and developed a calendar for kids that had events and activities that matched with key dates in their lives: for example, a set of special activities on one's birthday. I did this originally as a gift. But the idea caught on and was published several years in a row. Then I moved on to technology applications, environmental education, then social and civic education. In each case, I have resisted being typecast. Yet I have second-guessed myself often as to whether the approach I was taking to building myself as a professional was the right one. That day a few weeks ago, at the Education Association, when we discussed teacher leadership, was a day of affirmation. It really is okay, the approach I have taken, to go from one emphasis to another. You didn't know that the ideas presented at the meeting had that effect, did you?

Problems: Key Points from the Focus Groups

At Michigan State University College of Education

- Teacher leadership is one of a number of roles. Others include teacher as researcher, teacher as instructional expert, teacher as professional learner, and teacher as coordinator of school and community activities.

- The Teacher as Leaders Framework bears a striking resemblance to models of political efficacy. As such, it could be seen as grounded in principles of liberal democracy, which means relevance in indigenous communities will be a continuing challenge.

- The framework can also be viewed as a model for excellence in the teaching profession.

- The concept of structural barriers, that is, those standing in the way of teacher leadership, should be viewed as incorporating technical, hierarchical, resource, and cultural considerations.

- The current global preoccupation with standardization of curriculum and accountability through testing may negatively affect the professional capacity to nurture teacher leadership.

- The concept of teacher leadership implies the presence of leaders and followers in the teaching profession. Formalizing teacher leadership could lead to fragmentation in the profession and in schools.

At the Michigan Education Association

- The status of the teaching profession is of grave concern in Michigan.

- Major obstacles confront the concept of teacher leadership in the United States:

  The absence of a clear concept of teacher leadership fosters adversarial relationships between principals and teacher leaders, with the latter being seen, as a result, as trouble makers.

  Trail blazing is stressful, time consuming, and difficult—teacher leaders can become easily discouraged.

  Principals can easily speak the language of shared leadership but hang onto the status quo.

  People who are accustomed to having decisions made for them may have difficulty accepting the responsibilities that go with teacher leadership—as a consequence, they may too easily relinquish their rights.

  When teacher leaders demand resources, authority figures can feel threatened and so can some teacher colleagues, since resources are scarce—a condition that could inhibit the flowering of teacher leadership.

  The growing involvement of parents in schools creates extra demands from parents, which may be constraining for teacher leaders.

- Teachers everywhere lack a forum for exchanging leadership stories.

- Mentoring of young teachers provides a window of opportunity to develop and model teacher leadership concepts. The concept of mentoring needs to be explored in relation to teacher leadership.

- The networking aspect of the Teachers as Leaders Framework can be viewed in terms of workplace sociability—teacher leaders using social activity as a means of developing networks of support, communication channels, articulation of ideas, strategies for political influence, community building, and so forth. This is particularly significant because of the social needs of young professionals.

- Acceptance of the concept of teacher leadership leads naturally to the question of student leadership.

- Teacher leadership is real in Michigan schools, but it is not conceptualized and not formal.

- The concept of parallel leadership needs to be extended and its links to school improvement clarified.

At Northern Michigan College in Traverse City

- Parallel leadership is an attractive concept because it is not adversarial.

- Most schools contain pockets of greatness, but this does not necessarily enhance the status of the profession. If administrators do not offer recognition, the profession will receive little from the public. Furthermore, pockets of greatness usually imply inadequacies somewhere else, and this could cause divisiveness.

- The training of college professors contradicts principles of teacher leadership. University scholarship encourages questioning and cynicism and, therefore, discourages a culture of success. Universities can douse the flame of leadership when they should be igniting it.

- If teacher leadership is essentially a manifestation of interactivity, what are the implications for isolated teachers and part-time academics?

- The relevance of the newer technologies to the Teachers as Leaders Framework needs clarification.

- Teacher leaders who run into too many barriers either give up or leave the profession. Often these people become known as whiners, cynics, outsiders, or the disaffected. The concept of negative leadership may sometimes be brought about by the denial of authentic leadership opportunities.

- University leadership programs must change drastically. They need to be based on the principle of *inclusivity* (e.g., teacher leadership), and to encompass the three processes of organizational revitalization:

    schoolwide learning

    culture building

    shared approaches to pedagogy

- In the United States, at the moment, there is a perception in some quarters that the teaching profession is being subsumed in national politics centering on accountability, testing, and litigation.

- Leadership development needs to be approached on many fronts:

    Revamp university courses and professional training.

    Develop leadership around a school issue or need and through on-the-job, experiential learning.

    Cut across processes of organizational renewal, including schoolwide learning, culture building, and shared approaches to teaching, learning, and assessment.

At Novi in Southeast Michigan

- The development of teacher leadership in isolation from the principal's role, and without involvement in processes for holistic school improvement, may not be very purposeful.

- Suggestions for teacher leadership development:

Mentoring should encompass demonstrations of pedagogy in real-life situations.

Teacher leaders should engage in action that shows that their work is focused on ideals, not on operations.

Teacher leadership cannot be separated from communication processes that bring parents into the educative process.

There is a need to understand significant negatives, such as complaining teachers, assessment paranoia, and failing schools.

- Teacher leadership may be easier to practice in situations of disadvantage than in situations of abundance, because those with power in well-endowed schools want to maintain things as they are.

- Teacher leaders can use unions and professional associations and networks to promote the professionalism of teachers.

References

Abbott, W. (1966). *The documents of Vatican II*. New York: America Press.

Andersen Consulting Institute for Strategic Change. (1999). *The evolving role of executive leadership*. New York: Author.

Apple, M. W. (1992). *Teachers and texts: A political economy of class and gender relations in education*. New York: Routledge.

Argyris, C. (1993). *On organizational learning*. Cambridge, MA: Blackwell Business.

Argyris, C., & Schon, D. (1979). *Organizational learning: A theory of action perspective*. Cambridge, MA: Addison-Wesley.

Argyris, C., & Schon, D. (1996). *Organizational learning II: Theory, method and practice*. Cambridge, MA: Addison-Wesley.

Avolio, B. J., & Bass, B. (1988). Transformational leadership, charisma and beyond. In J. G. Hunt, B. Baliga, H. Dachler, & C. Schriesheim (Eds.), *Emerging Leadership Vistas* (pp. 29-49). Lanham, MD: Lexington Books.

Bates, R. (1983). *Educational administration and the management of knowledge*. Waurn Ponds, Victoria, Australia: Deakin Press.

Bates, R. (1992, July). *Leadership and school culture*. Paper presented at the Interuniversity Congress of the Organization of Teaching Faculty of Philosophy and Science, Seville, Spain.

Beare, H. (2001). *Creating the future school: Student outcomes and the reform of education*. London: Routledge/Falmer.

Beatty, B. (2000). The emotions of educational leadership: Breaking the silence. *International Journal of Leadership in Education, 3*(4), 331–358.

Blackmore, J. (1996). Doing 'emotional labour' in the education market place: Stories from the field of women in management. *Discourse: Studies in the Cultural Politics of Education, 17*(3), 337-349.

Bolman, L., & Deal, T. (1994). Looking for leadership: Another search party's report. *Educational Administration Quarterly, 30*(1), 77-96.

Boomer, G. (1985). A celebration of teaching. *Australian Teacher, 11,* 13-20.

Bryk, A. S., & Schneider, B. (1996). *Social trust: A moral resource for school improvement.* Chicago: University of Chicago, Center for School Improvement.

Caldwell, B. (1992). The principal as leader of the self-managing school in Australia. *Journal of Educational Administration, 30*(3), 6–19.

Carnegie Forum on Education and the Economy. (1986). *A nation prepared: Teachers for the 21st century: The report on the Task Force on Teaching as a Profession.* New York: Author.

Clark, K. E., & Clark, M. B. (1994). *Choosing to lead.* Charlotte, NC: Irongate Press.

Coleman, J. S. (1966). *Equality of educational opportunity.* Washington, DC: Government Printing Office.

Congregation for Catholic Education. (1998). *The Catholic school on the threshold of the third millennium.* Homebush, Australia: St. Paul Publications.

Conley, S., & Muncey, D. (1999). Teachers talk about teaming and leadership in their work. *Theory Into Practice, 38*(1), 46-55.

Crowther, F. (1996). Teacher leadership: Explorations in theory and practice. *Leading and Managing, 2*(4), 304–321.

Crowther, F., Andrews, D., Dawson, M., & Lewis, M. (2001). *IDEAS Facilitation Folder.* Brisbane, Australia: Queensland Department of Education.

Crowther, F., Hann, L., & McMaster, J. (2001). Leadership. In P. Cuttance, *School innovation: Pathway to the knowledge society.* Canberra, Australia: Australian Commonwealth Department of Education, Training and Youth Affairs.

Crowther, F., & Olsen, P. (1996). *Teachers as leaders: An exploration of success stories in socio-economic disadvantaged communities.* Brisbane, Australia: Department of Education.

Cuttance, P. (2001). *School innovation: Pathway to the knowledge society.* Canberra, Australia: Australian Commonwealth Department of Education, Training and Youth Affairs.

Darling-Hammond, L. (1997). *The right to learn: A blueprint for creating schools that work.* San Francisco: Jossey-Bass.

Day, C. (2000). Effective leadership and reflective practice. *Reflective Practice, 1*(1), 113-127.

Day, C., & Bakioglu, A. (1996). Development and disenchantment in the professional lives of head teachers. In I. Goodson & A. Hargreaves (Eds.), *Teachers' professional lives* (pp. 205-227). New York: Falmer.

De Pree, M. (1997). *Leading without power: Finding hope in serving community.* San Francisco: Jossey-Bass.

Dinham, S., & Scott, C. (1997). *The teacher 2000 project: A study of teacher motivation and health.* New South Wales, Australia: University of Western Sydney-Nepean.

Drucker, P. (1994). The age of social transformation. *Atlantic Monthly, 274*(5), 53-80.

Duignan, P., & Macpherson, R. J. S. (1992). Creating new knowledge about educative leadership. In P. Duignan & R. J. S. Macpherson (Eds.), *Educative leadership: A practical theory for new administrators and managers* (pp. 1-17). Lewes, Australia: Falmer.

Education Commission of the States Task Force on Education for Economic Growth. (1983). *Action for excellence.* Denver, CO: Author.

Fleming, G. L., & Leo, T. (2000, April). *The role of trust building in its relation to teacher efficacy.* Paper presented at the Symposium at the American Educational Research Association 2000, New Orleans, Louisiana.

Flynn, M. (1979). *Catholic schools and the communication of faith.* Homebush, Australia: St. Paul Publications.

Forster, E. (1997). Teacher leadership: Professional right and responsibility. *Action in Teacher Education, 19*(3), 82-94.

Glickman, C. (1998). Educational leadership for democratic purpose: What do we mean? *International Journal of Leadership in Education, 1*(1), 47-53.

Goldberg, M. (2000, September). Leadership for change: An interview with John Goodlad. *Phi Delta Kappan,* 82-85.

Goleman, D. (1998). What makes a leader? *Harvard Business Review, 76*(6), 93-103.

Gronn, P. (1999). *The making of educational leaders.* Management and Leadership in Education Series. London: Cassell.

Gutierrez, K., Rymes, B., & Larson, J. (1995). Script, counterscript, and underlife in the classroom: James Brown versus Brown and the Board of Education. *Harvard Educational Review, 65*(3), 445-471.

Hallinger, P., & Heck, R. (1996). Reassessing the principal's role in school effectiveness: A review of empirical research, 1980–1995. *Education Administration Quarterly, 32*(1), 5-45.

Hambrick, D. C. (1989, Summer). Guest editor's introduction: Putting top managers back in the strategy picture. *Journal of Strategic Management* [Special Issue], 5-15.

Handy, C. (1994). *The empty raincoat: Making sense of the future.* London: Hutchinson Press.

Handy, C. (1996). The new language of organizing and its implications for leaders. In F. Hesselbein, M. Goldsmith, & R. Beckhard (Eds.), *The leader of the future* (pp. 3-10). San Francisco: Jossey-Bass.

Hargreaves, A. (1994). Changing work cultures of teaching. In F. Crowther & B. Caldwell (Eds.), *The workplace in education: Australian per-*

spectives. Australian Council Educational Administration Yearbook. Sydney: Edward Arnold.

Hargreaves, A., Earl, L., Moore, S., & Manning, S. (2001). *Learning to change: Teaching beyond subjects and standards*. San Francisco: Jossey-Bass/Wiley.

Hargreaves, A., & Fink, D. (2000). Three dimensions of educational reform. *Educational Leadership, 57*(7), 30-34.

Hargreaves, A., & Goodson, I. (1996). Teachers' professional lives: Aspirations and actualities. In I. Goodson & A. Hargreaves (Eds.), *Teachers' professional lives* (pp. 1-27). New York: Falmer.

Heenan, D., & Bennis, W. (1999). *Co-leaders: The power of great partnerships*. New York: Wiley.

Heifetz, R., & Laurie, D. (1997, January/February). The work of leadership. *Harvard Business Review, 75*(1), 124–134.

Holmes Group. (1986). *Tomorrow's teachers: A Report of the Holmes Group*. East Lansing, MI: Author.

Hoy, W. K., & Miskel, C. G. (1991). *Educational administration: Theory, research and practice* (4th ed.). New York: McGraw-Hill.

Ingvarson, L., & Chadbourne, R. (1996). The rise and fall of the advanced skills teacher in Australia. *Leading and Managing, 2*(1), 49-69.

Kaagan, S. (1999). *Leadership games: Experiential learning for organizational development*. Thousand Oaks, CA: Sage.

Kanter, R. (1994, July/August). Collaborative advantage: The art of alliances. *Harvard Business Review, 72*(4), 96-108.

Katz, D., & Kahn, R. L. (1966). *The social psychology of organizations*. New York: Wiley.

Katzenmeyer, M., & Moller, G. (1996). *Awakening the sleeping giant: Leadership development for teachers*. Thousand Oaks, CA: Corwin.

King, B., and Newmann, F. (1999). *School capacity as a goal for professional development: Mapping the terrain in low-income schools*. Paper presented at the Annual Meeting of AERA, Montreal.

King, B., & Newmann, F. (2000, April). Will teacher learning advance school goals? *Phi Delta Kappan, 81*(8), 576-580.

Kofman, F., & Senge, P. (1993). Communities of commitment: The heart of learning organizations. *Organizational Dynamics, 22*(2), 4-23.

Lakomski, G. (1995). Leadership and learning: From transformational leadership to organizational learning. *Leading and Managing, 1*(3), 211-225.

Leithwood, K. (1994). Leadership for school restructuring. *Educational Administration Quarterly, 30*(4), 498-518.

Leithwood, K., & Jantzi, D. (1998, April). *Distributed leadership and student engagement in school*. Paper presented at the Annual Meeting of the American Educational Research Association, San Diego, California.

Leithwood, K., Jantzi, D., Ryan, S., & Steinbach, R. (1997, March). *Distributed leadership in secondary schools*. Paper presented at the Annual Meeting of the American Educational Research Association, Chicago, Illinois.

Lieberman, A., Saxl, E., & Miles, M. (1988). Teachers' leadership: Ideology and practice. In A. Lieberman (Ed.), *Building a professional culture in schools* (pp. 148-166). New York: Teachers College Press.

Limerick, D., Cunnington, B., & Crowther, F. (1998). *Managing the new organization: Collaboration and sustainability in the post-corporate world*. Warriewood, Australia: Business & Professional Publishing.

Little, J. W. (1995). Contested ground: The basis of teacher leadership in two restructuring high schools. *Elementary School Journal, 96*(1), 47-63.

Lortie, D. (1975). *Schoolteacher: A sociological study*. Chicago: University of Chicago Press.

Louis, K., Marks, H. M., and Kruse, S. (1996). Teachers' professional community in restructuring schools. *American Educational Research Journal, 33* (4), 757-798.

Macquarie Library. (1998). *Macquarie dictionary* (3rd ed.). Sydney, Australia: Macquarie University.

Mayer, J. A. (1943). *Max Weber and German politics*. London: Faber & Faber.

Mintzberg, H. (1994/January-February). The fall and rise of strategic planning. *Harvard Business Review,* 107-114.

Muncey, D., & McQuillan, P. (1996). *Reform and resistance in schools and classroom:. An ethnographic view of the coalition of essential schools*. New Haven, CT: Yale University Press.

Newmann, F., & Wehlage, G. (1995). *Successful school restructuring: A report to the public and educators*. Madison: Center on Organization and Restructuring of Schools, University of Wisconsin.

Nirenberg, J. (1993). *The living organization: Transforming teams into work place communities*. Homewood, IL: Business One Irwin.

O'Neill, J. (1995). On schools as learning organizations: A conversation with Peter Senge. *Educational Leadership, 52*(7), 20-23.

Padilla, R., Trevino, J., Gonzalez, K., & Trevino, J. (1996, April). *The unfolding matrix: A dialogical technique for qualitative data acquisition and analysis*. Demonstration presented at the Annual Meeting of the American Educational Research Association, New York, New York.

Ponder, G. A., & Holmes, K. M. (2000). Purpose, products and visions: The creation of new schools. *The Educational Forum, 56*(4), 405-418.

Pounder, D. G., Ogawa, R. T., & Adams, E. A. (1995). Leadership as an organization-wide phenomenon: Its impact on school performance. *Educational Administration Quarterly, 31*(4), 564–588.

Rice, E. M., and Schneider, G. T. (1994). A decade of teacher empowerment: An empirical analysis of teacher involvement in decision making, 1980-1991. *Journal of Educational Administration, 32*(1), 43-58.

Rizvi, F. (1992). Educative leadership in a multicultural society. In P. Duignan & R. J. S. McPherson (Eds.), *Educative leadership: A practical theory for new administrators and managers* (pp. 134-170). Lewes, Australia: Falmer.

Sachs, J. (2000). Rethinking the practice of teacher professionalism. In C. Day, A. Fernandez, T. Hauge, & J. Moller (Eds.), *The life and work of teachers: International perspectives in changing times.* London: Routledge/Falmer.

Schein, E. (1992). *Organizational culture and leadership.* San Francisco: Jossey-Bass.

Schon, D. (1983). *The reflective practitioner: How professionals think in action.* New York: Basic Books.

Senge, P. (1992). *The fifth discipline: The art and practice of the learning organization.* New York: Doubleday.

Senge, P. (1997, September/October). Communities of leaders and learners. *Harvard Business Review,* 30-31.

Senge, P. (2000). *Schools that learn.* New York: Doubleday.

Sergiovanni, T. (1998). Leadership as pedagogy, capital development and school effectiveness. *International Journal of Leadership in Education: Theory and Practice, 1*(1), 37–46.

Sergiovanni, T. (2000). *The lifeworld of leadership.* San Francisco: Jossey-Bass.

Sherrill, J. (1999). Preparing teachers for leadership roles in the 21st century. *Theory Into Practice, 38*(1), 56-61.

Shor, I., & Freire, P. (1987). *A pedagogy for liberation: Dialogues on transforming education.* New York: Bergin & Garvey.

Sinclair, A. (1995). The seduction of the self-managed team and the re-invention of the team-as-a-group. *Leading and Managing, 1*(1), 44-60.

Smith, W., & Ellett, C. (2000, April). *Reconceptualizing school leadership for the 21st century: Music, metaphors and leadership density.* Paper presented at the Annual Meeting of the American Educational Research Association, New Orleans, Louisiana.

Spillane, J. P., Halverson, R., & Diamond, J. B. (2001). Investigating school leadership practice: A distributed perspective. *Educational Researcher, 30*(3), 23-28.

Troman, G., & Woods, P. (2001). *Primary teachers' stress.* London: RoutledgeFalmer.

Waller, W. (1932). *The sociology of teaching.* New York: Russell & Russell.

Index

CORWIN
PRESS

The Corwin Press logo—a raven striding across an open book—represents the happy union of courage and learning. We are a professional-level publisher of books and journals for K–12 educators, and we are committed to creating and providing resources that embody these qualities. Corwin's motto is "Success for All Learners."